Breakup

Science Backed Steps to Getting Over Your Ex Fast

(How to Deal With Your Ex After a Breakup by Using the No Contact Rule Breakupbreakupbreakup)

Ruben Feliciano

Published By **Chris David**

Ruben Feliciano

Breakup: Science Backed Steps to Getting Over Your Ex Fast (How to Deal With Your Ex After a Breakup by Using the No Contact Rule Breakupbreakupbreakup)

ISBN   978-1-998927-28-9

No part of this guidebook shall be reproduced in any form without permission in writing from the publisher except in the case of brief quotations embodied in critical articles or reviews.

Legal & Disclaimer

Table Of Contents

Chapter 1: Determine the Reason of the Break-up

Remember the ones fairy memories wherein the prince marries his stunning princess and live fortunately ever after?

The problem with the ones recollections is that they do no longer supply us a glimpse of techniques the protagonists' marriage have emerge as out. From this, we will claim that being in a dating is enough purpose to love existence and possibly end up the happiest man or woman within the international.

But the reality is that the entirety is subjected under instances.

At one issue in the destiny, your relationship can every flip for the high-quality or skew to the worst.

In some failed relationships, every companions have a tendency responsible each different for such a number of outstanding motives. What complicates that is that neither one is going to offer in. Ego has its vicinity in everyone, and in such times as a harm-up, they become too controlling.

In the event of a break-up, your ego is the least you can rely upon. Instead, try and look at yourself similarly in your accomplice. Try to factor out your flaws and connect them with the situation you are in now. What led you so far?

And from this, we are able to maintain to information the reasons. Now, they take many paperwork. There are reasons that can be logical, and however there are others which can be within the bounds of exaggeration.

Examining every one takes you a step towards overcoming the smash-up and into reuniting together together with your large different.

Habits

A lot of relationships capsize thru awful behavior. Maybe your partner is an incessant gambler, or you're a chronic smoker who shuns reprimands.

Whatever the case, behavior play a element in sabotaging relationships out of annoyance or health troubles. We can all say that too much playing or smoking can be unstable. But a number of us will preserve stubbornly on to those behavior amidst threats of a harm-up. Your companion can also have definitely been very worried with you, and possibly it's miles of their notion that breaking aside with you may be the quality remedy and preference that they have to make you quit your addiction. But reputedly, it in reality is not the remarkable.

Communication

Anyone can agree that verbal exchange performs a function inside the development of any dating however it could moreover become the preamble to a downfall.

Relationships start off easy. Communication on this section is not a first rate deal of a hassle. But given enough time, you can thoroughly encounter a few obstacles.

It gets complicated while both of you try and carry the worst from each unique. And this stems from constant arguing approximately petty subjects.

Verbal squabbles are herbal. But left unchecked, each of you may come to a point of quitting when you have obtain your tolerance diploma.

Personal Space

Cooperation is one of many essentialities in a dating. In order for it to work, each of you'll need to meet every one among a type's needs and confront every specific's issues. But there will come that intense component wherein each of you would flow as a ways as controlling your partner.

At times, too much manage in truth subverts your accomplice's interests, primary to even extra troubles. During the ones instances, the superb solution is to provide every different the non-public region that they need. When denied of this, breakup may be obvious when one feels limited.

Don't be Needy

After the break-up, you can enjoy as regardless of the fact that you're at fault. We typically usually have a tendency to companion awful matters that arise to us with non-public duty.

We can blame ourselves at one thing, however it does now not do hundreds while we emerge as too determined.

Certainly, we would go to intense lengths simply to get interest. During a smash-up, the least you could do is to re-plant your self to your ex's mind.

Instead of having the 2 of you returned together over again, if you switch out to be needy, your efforts will great worsen the huge rift amongst you and your ex.

But we couldn't clearly break out from this temptation. As the harm-up starts offevolved to take an emotional toll, you'll need to find out approaches at the manner to replenish that void for your coronary heart.

Apparently, there are methods to try this at the same time as now not having to undergo emotions of natural desperation.

Take your Time

Let's face it. You although love your ex, a lot so that you are doing a little issue it takes to resuscitate the union.

Again, this worsens the state of affairs. Your ex can exceptional see your desperation and the manner you simply cannot pass on living without her spherical.

Instead, attempt to take the destroy-up with a rational mind-set. This includes searching for to beautify your self and understand the issues that induced the ruin-up.

If it way plenty to you to restore the relationship, you need to recollect having to attend till topics begin to calm down. During this time, combat off any temptation to reflect onconsideration on your ex and cognizance on readying yourself for the large comeback alternatively.

Chapter 2: Show do now not Tell

Do not try and textual content, e mail or name your ex beneath any events! Attempting to influence her that you may trade and that you can be a higher boyfriend. This is truely an instance of the way decided you are, and it's going to fine purpose your ex to move on plenty a lot less complex.

Try plenty as to never guarantee some component. Chances are you may not be capable of live up to your ex's expectancies.

During the ruin-up, make an effort to make first-class adjustments in your self. Quit or restriction certain behavior and stay every day as you normally may also.

Your ex may additionally recognize from your buddies that you are willing to beautify yourself whilst now not having to trouble her with hazy promises.

Never communicate approximately the Break-up

One carnal component to do not forget is to by no means mention your separation.

Whether you're collectively together with your friends or family, by no means try to convey up any communicate concerning the harm-up. Again, this could exceptional display how prone you are under the weight of your non-public emotions. Having this mind-set suggests which you aren't however prepared to get again on the proper tune.

If humans ask you the way you are doing after the destroy-up, inform them which you are doing terrific and which you wish your ex is doing outstanding as nicely. Nothing extra than that.

Stay casual and live calm. You are in no favorable function to whine or beg. Let time heal and allow your feelings be given a while.

Be Mysterious

Ever thinking about that day one of the aftermath, each of you will wonder, "How is my ex doing?"

Throughout the destroy-up, each of you are attempting tough not to speak with every awesome. It is a transitional duration of letting the temperature slide all of the way down to tolerable degrees. This is a time on the identical time as anger problems are being confronted and the spite for each other is subsiding.

It is in this 2nd that your communication strains along with your ex are in brief lessen-off so as not to intervene with the duration of "emotional recuperation." Considering this, it is satisfactory that you would possibly need to be incognito for a while and allow your ex maintain on guessing. Always preserve in thoughts thriller equals appeal.

Go "Underground"

You can try this with the beneficial useful resource of proscribing your get right of get entry to to in your social media debts, and this shows restricting your Facebook wall posts and tweets. If you actually have that itch to share every element of your each day existence, achieve this in a preferred manner. Never positioned up some aspect, whether or not or not in an specific or implicit manner, regarding the destroy-up. This manner, you can keep away from giving your self off all of the whilst tickle your ex's hobby.

Sensing the Signs

Your ex's interest will best broaden wider on the same time as you keep up going underground for some time. The temptation to understand urges her to get right of get entry to to important property of information.

Your pals or family can also additionally serve as a relay tool. Your ex will try to ask them how you are doing or whether or not you are trying to transport on. This is a reality!

For accurate degree, attempt no longer to feed your friends or family too much information either. Again, provide very hazy solutions that couldn't be deciphered effects. If a person out of your carefully-knit circle of friends asks, "How are you taking all this in?" sincerely solution with "Fine" or "I'm doing properly."

Such answers are open to interpretation, however this intrigues your ex even greater.

Emotions in Motion

Remember that a destroy-up is most effective a transitory second if you however have mind on getting lower back on your ex.

You though have that affection and you're yearning intimacy, which your ex can also try to suppress.

But we couldn't good buy the opportunity that she can be experiencing the identical emotional void you experience. Your ex also can want to satisfy nice questions.

Not letting your ex discover how you are feeling at some diploma in the break-up is an crucial technique. Staying incognito for goodbye will supply her enough time to rethink having you as a companion. Understand as time goes via using people start to think less of the harm, anger and bad feelings and greater of what modified into top, imparting you allow for a strong duration of no touch. Women need time to surprise approximately you, supply her that. With you staying reclusive and restricting your online and bodily presence, your ex will find out how splendid it's miles with out you inside the image.

There will be times wherein your ex is awfully lacking you. The possibility of getting again together can also actually be over the horizon.

Your harm file

The subsequent step is the harm document. Get easy about this and be honest! What did you do or say that could have a horrible impact for your future dating? Did you perform a little aspect you've got been liable for? Did you cheat on her? If that is the case, she have become right to unload you. There can be no experience in begging her, you may ought to trade if you actually need her

15

again and you may ought to reveal yourself to her.

In my experience, 99% of the time the fellow overpressures the female, inflicting her to fall out of love due to susceptible, insecure and needy behavior. Masculine strength is not submissive or unsure. It is about motive, pressure, being purpose orientated, direct and fantastic. Uncertainty and submissiveness is a feminine extraordinary and a girl needs you to be greater of man than she is.

Most possibly you possibly did the same.

The greater you confirmed of your prone and insecure component, the greater your ex will make you pay for it. She will take a look at you, the greater you messed up, the more difficult and longer the checks is probably. But you may be prepared for this. If you cried, begged, blew up her cellular telephone or referred to as her pals, it's going to get quite horrible, she can be able to make you pay.

The easy element can be to get her to reevaluate you. The hard aspect is probably to get a one-of-a-type rate than final time. You can look at this collectively together with your grocery shopping for, if you have to pick out among specific merchandise, you're making your selection quite quick. The rest of the time you will be seeking out evidence that you have made the proper preference. It is unusual to admit that you formerly made an errors in judgement.

You don't have to be similar to you were at the same time as to procure to apprehend her, you need to be better, now not a pleaser but a higher model of your self. You ought to be on the very exceptional she has ever visible you!

In this step you want to be clean about the errors you have made. This includes susceptible behavior inside the past and at some point of the ruin-up. Take be aware about inclined behavior and actively attempt to restore it within the destiny. Get rid of your fear of being left.

Chapter 3: Find your masculine center

You ought to define your masculinity yet again. Find that internal warrior of yours. Take your pride lower lower back, straighten up and stroll upright, regardless of what comes your way.

At any given detail for your relationship you want your female to have a take a look at you, now not the alternative way round.

It is in her nature to observe you, you are the strong chief and you are making the selections. This doesn't exchange. Take a chunk of paper and write down the tendencies you would like to undertake, the list may additionally encompass the subsequent:

●decisive

●direct

●truthful

- outgoing

- daring

- hazard taking

- captivating

- and so on.

Whatever you would love to embody, simply list it. From now on assessment this list, attempt to put in force as some of the person tendencies to your every day lifestyles as viable and workout them. I understand you want to get your ex once more, however you have to understand, which you need to permit go of this concept. Women are chasing while you, you have severa alternatives, so that you by no means chase after one lady.

You are chasing your reason. You have matters to accomplish to your life, and being a boyfriend is not really considered one of them. That is a bi product your truely being notable.

She want to chase whilst you, she should try to persuade you that she might be the brilliant choice for you.

I realise this seems like proper far from the stone age however it's far a reality. Practice your masculinity again. Coach Corey Wayne uses the analogy that the person is much like the mountain. The female is mom nature, now every now and then mom nature might also additionally additionally shine on the mountain in all her lovable glory, but different times she also can batter the mountain with showers of rain, hail and violent tempestuous winds. However, regardless of what, the mountain does not go with the flow. It is someone's mission to be the mountain, sturdy and company in his beliefs, his picks, in his masculine center. Never wavering regardless of what's thrown at him. This is masculine power and masculine electricity draws a girl female.

You will ought to take a look at the subsequent pointers to get the most out of it:

●physical exercising at least 3 times each week

●eat at the least 1 pound of vegetables an afternoon (preferably green)

●don't overindulge in sexual people of the circle of relatives or immoderate masturbating

●socialize with new people, decorate your social abilties

●exercising flirting competencies with girls

You need to pick up things you sacrificed to your relationship, revisit your interests and passions. To accomplish these small topics will broaden yourself belief.

Countless research screen that self notion is the primary trait girls discover most appealing about a person.

Physical workout will need to come to be a routine, whether or not or not you want it or not. You will look extra younger, more active and sense better. In aggregate with the wholesome weight-reduction plan, which ought to encompass as a minimum a pound of ideally dark leafy vegetables, fruit works as well. This will make your skin glow, you can sleep better and lots less. People will start to notice this after spherical 30 days.

Get out and socialize like never in advance than. Go out on dates, talk to random human beings you meet. Not simply the lovely girls or lady in cutting-edge, however to each person. Practice your social skills whenever, everywhere feasible! Try to grow to be a great conversationalist, I recommend analyzing

Dale Carnegie's 'How to win friends and effect humans'.

In elegant, this means to invite the right questions, in particular with women. If you attempt to win them over and display your self to them, they'll most effective get became off via your neediness and approval looking for behavior.

Give them the danger to show themselves to you. To earn your interest. Match and replicate their interest, there may be not anything that turns a woman more off than if she realizes which you are extra into her than she is into you.

Another fantastic tip is this one:

"Read her actions, now not her terms!" How frequently has a girl has been requested what she desires in someone, but the man she ultimately ends up with isn't always some thing as described. Always be privy to a female's moves now not her phrases. Women vote with their feet. If she is continuously calling, texting, touching and seeking to be spherical you, then she can not be eliminating you.

Chapter 4: Fake it, until you make it!

It can be very vital so that you can understand what ladies certainly try to tell you. Therefore, you need to select out her actions, now not her phrases.

When your female pal cautioned you, she didn't want to lose you, or which you are such an incredible character, she didn't suggest that. Her movements showed the very contrary, she preferred you out of her life. Sure, she cared for you, but she avoids telling you the reality because of the fact she is aware of it'll harm you, on pinnacle of that have you ever left a susceptible impact, making her accept as authentic with you couldn't take it.

When she tells you which you aren't paying attention to her, it doesn't suggest you don't pay attention her, but you aren't interested by her lifestyles. You are not paying enough hobby to the statistics of her life and her tales to don't forget them.

You don't ask about modern-day-day subjects she has taking location. Often at the same time as a lady comes home and complains approximately her bitchy boss at artwork or something mundane occasion she encountered that day, someone being cause orientated immediately attempts to repair and clear up all her troubles, supplying solutions. She does no longer want answers, she simply needs you to zip it, nod your head and concentrate to her! Women get thru their problems via virtually speakme about them. So, simply suck it up, shut up and pay interest. A trick I rent myself is to invite my lady, 'Babe do you want my advice? Or do you clearly want me to listen?' You also can find that conversation leads to a a hit cease in the mattress room.

When she tells you that you don't spend sufficient time collectively together with her, or too much time together along with your friends, she doesn't want you to spend extra time collectively together together with her, but more excessive first-rate time. Men are pretty easy minded. If you hold my existence nowadays, I can be dependable to you for the relaxation of my existence.

If you practice this to a lady it'd pass like this: in case you keep her life every day, she might be dependable to you for the relaxation of her lifestyles. She doesn't hold music of the belongings you probable did for her some years in the beyond. The instances you took her out. Women stay within the 2d, she desires to feel, to experience your actual affection each day. And this affection isn't always verified by the use of blowing up her mobile cellphone. Because what you really did thru over pursuing her changed into egocentric. You didn't act out of affection, you acted out of worry. You have been scared to be left.

We men are happy with the equal matters each day. A girl can't be. She has to experience all the shades of the rainbow, and she or he has to revel in them with you. You want to make her chuckle, cry, indignant and jealous all together. Do you maintain in thoughts an incident whilst your ex tried to reason a combat for no motive? You see? She modified into seeking to get you to act up. To get up, to make her enjoy alive.

She will bear in mind you with the aid of the intensity and the positivity of the feelings she had while she changed into with you. Make her experience desired and preferred each 2d. As rapid as you're long past, you attention to your desires. She can't be the goal and motive of your life.

Let her pursue you, don't chase after a woman. I generally listen guys that got screwed over thru a female say: "They simply constantly fall for assholes and finesse chicks (a woman who makes use of you for what you have got)."

That isn't right, however a person who treats a woman poorly stands up for himself. She can chase him and show her social fee to him.

If you deliver her all your affection for gratis she cannot respect it.

Now that you have had a few perception into the female mind, try to examine this facts. Talk to human beings anywhere. Develop remarkable social skills.

Do this with human beings of all age and gender. This will prepare you. Once you're going through a adorable lady, it's going to no longer intimidate you anymore, because you are used to talking to strangers.

Always apprehend your self as a exceptional capture. If you don't be given as actual with it in reality but, faux it, till you're making it. Try to behave love it, humans will respond as a result. Build your self guarantee till you simply recollect it.

This is a very easy but powerful trick. Our thoughts works just like a circuit switch. Once you agree with you've got superb trends, for example extraordinary flirting skills, you really are perceived via way of others to have them.

Most ladies are interested by assured guys, you don't ought to be a jerk to be confident, however you have to recognize what you need and choose it unapologetically. During the first 30 days, there could be days whilst you don't pay attention from any of your pals or ladies you picked up. Keep your head up, be busy collectively along with your new obligations, faux to be assured even in case you don't in truth experience locate it not possible to withstand. Get to be had, make new friends, emerge as extra social, this can enhance your self assurance.

A little trick to carry out this is the "flirt with the arena" trick, as I call it. You want to fall in love with the complete global. Instead of seeing enemies anywhere you want to count on of every human as a part of your family. Be excellent, be direct, don't do small communicate. If you behave like this, even though no one responds on the begin, you may quickly see the adjustments. Become the change you want to see in the worldwide.

People will deal with you in any other case, they may healthful and replicate your behavior toward you... If you communicate to all people you can beautify your social talents rapid!

Like I stated, it doesn't remember who you're talking to, as long as you are interacting as lots as feasible.

Chapter 5: Don't recognition on the outcome!

As we defined in Step 4: Find your masculine center, it is within the nature of someone to take risks, to take the step into uncertainty.

This applies not handiest to excessive situations, but moreover to normal existence. Especially inside the interplay among you and distinct ladies. You need to take the hazard that she would possibly probably reject you. You aren't fixated on her; your vanity does not rely on the judgement of every extraordinary character.

If you are direct and get without delay to the factor with out being impolite, you obtained't display worry or worry over the very last results. The trick hereby is to live without a doubt inside the present. You don't want your mind to wander off into the destiny, what might possibly take region, what effects you would probably face. That is a waste of time and strength. You have to live within the second, act as you revel in really now.

This manner moreover upon interaction with a very adorable woman, you must in no way reflect onconsideration on the future. Don't take into account if she might also moreover offer you along with her variety, or how it'd be to undress her. This will demanding you up, and you can automatically invest extra into her than she has invested into you.

Like we already protected, deliver her location to show herself to you. She has to recognize that a few strive is needed to bypass your clean out, and that she may be proud if she did that. Flip the script guys and start seeing yourself because the prize.

Don't concentrate to those choose out-up artists that attempt to manipulate girls. This has not a few aspect to do with it. But it has everything to do with you finding your masculine middle and acting sturdy and assured.

Be clearly open for the very last outcomes, she might also wonder you.

Don't even consider getting her range. A high-quality way to exercising this is to speak to girls you physical discover attractive. You want to let them understand that you like them, but then you will turn round and walk away.

This will improve yourself notion another time and depart an imprint on your thoughts. Let circulate. Don't overthink and over complicate subjects.

Just begin with the resource of pronouncing hi there to strangers. If you don't dare to perform that, reflect onconsideration on it, would likely you rather have a person anticipate poorly of you, or need to anticipate poorly approximately your self because of the fact you didn't dare to look at thru?

But, don't be that fool that sticks to a girl like glue, totally fixated on her hoping he would possibly rating. Circulate, be amusing to be round. Talk to ladies and let them flow all over again.

Remember even in case you don't experience like studying new humans, mainly girls, this could help you relatively to get your ex once more! Women do have a experience for a way properly you rating with exclusive Women. A guy who's a achievement with different girls is someone to be desired, men need to be you and women need to be with you. Even if girls commonly generally generally tend to behave as if jealousy is a few component to keep away from, it's far hidden hobby and admiration. The peer evaluations you get from brilliant women, who are all very opposition driven with reference to men, is distinctly important.

Picture this situation: you go to a club with a few pals. Everything goes first-rate, you act clean with the women, bypass out proper compliments, flirt, and go away in advance than they will be able to genuinely entice you. Making yourself interesting at first and then scarce. Just so it occurs, there has been a chum of your ex, and he or she noticed all that.

Be assured that your ex will realize this via the subsequent morning. You can also moreover quick be paying attention to approximately it.

But you may't stress this approach, once more faux it, until you are making it, but attempt to encompass it. This is a long way beyond truly getting some different chance with your lady pal.

You want to use this principle with all of the girls in your life, they have to in no way get sufficient of you. Make them hooked on you, as quickly as they begin getting worried, pull lower back on the same tempo she is pursuing you. Remember this principle...Two steps in advance, one step decrease again, all the on the identical time as though progressing.

To end up extraordinary at this, it takes exercise. For me, for a few weeks I challenged myself to get at the least one smartphone huge variety a day! I recognize you want to not be very last outcomes centered, however as you get higher ladies will make it honestly smooth for you, or perhaps provide their amount.

This works mainly nicely in case you flow into and meet a woman you already talked to, but didn't ask for her variety. By that factor, you have got were given already verified to her that you are not a prone beta male and you could manipulate a lady like her, and that is a incredible function to be in.

One problem to be aware of is that this, the sexual tension you enjoy inside the starting will ultimately put on off. You gets caught in buddy area in case you don't improvement and pressure the easy escalation of the situation. This approach at least via the use of the zero.33 time you meet a girl, you need to invite her out. The greater you increase in self assure you can short be capable of strike up a conversation with a girl and have a particular date set together along side her internal a manner of minutes earlier than even changing numbers.

Chapter 6: The Reunion Date

The Preparation Phase If you obtain dumped

By this time, your conversation lines are open all over again. It's critical that you do now not popularity on a dating but focus on learning every awesome all another time and constructing chemistry this may result in the each of you turning into snug round each exceptional for the second time.

It grow to be installation in advance that in case you've got been dumped you should no longer contact you ex in any respect. If and even as she reaches out to you first, experience loose to invite her out. You want to be very careful with this even though. If you want to transport on a date together together together with your ex all over again, you want to start thru using asking her out in a non-threatening, basically platonic way. Do not skip on 'friendship' dates which incorporates lunch dates or going out for coffee, plan fun filled, romantic dates within the night time time thru wherein you can expand chemistry and increase enchantment all over again.

If your ex-female pal does no longer agree to head on a date you want to reply. 'No issues, if you trade your mind offer me a call, I'd love to look you. I need to get going, bye.' Or rephrase to your very non-public words then get off the cellphone and pass approximately your industrial corporation. This is vitally vital. You are sexually and romantically inquisitive about this female so act find it irresistible. Do now not ever play the placement of a chum that is the fastest way to getting hurt the second one time round. Be direct and smooth for your intentions which you most effective have romantic hobby in her, either she is inclined to exit or now not.

If she isn't, you genuinely talk what you need in a loving and respectful way, depart your door open to her and keep to cognizance on being the satisfactory you. If after two times she has reached out to you she even though refuses to set a particular date, then you absolutely prevent mentioning the concept of having together until she does. Keep the verbal exchange to not much less than five mins or less then get off the telephone and maintain it shifting. What you are speakme via your moves is that you are a assured man who's aware of what he dreams, that you could not take transport of much less and if she is not willing to reciprocate interest then you may be moving on together with your existence until you meet that individual who does.

The Preparation Phase If you dumped them

The dynamics are barely distinct here. If you dumped them, in this situation exceptional is it appropriate so that you may be the primary one to reap out and make contact with them first. Call them, express regret for being a dick and offer an reason for which you are sorry and would like to see them. Yes, you could need to perform a little ass kissing however proper day, ultimately you are the one who kicked them to the size down.

If it's a yes, best! Plan a fun crammed romantic date, all over again do no longer attention on a dating or locking her proper right down to a dedication, just genuinely have a terrific time. If she says no, another time you certainly reply 'No issues, in case you exchange your thoughts deliver me a name, I'd want to appearance you. I have to get going, bye.' And you drift on and never touch yet again until she contacts you first.

If there can be any spark of romance left, then she will be able to have no 2d mind about pronouncing "YES". The secret's to make an offer that she really can't refuse. That provide is being the exceptional version of you.

6 Do's and Don'ts Out On A Date

You eventually have been given her to mention positive to exit on a date with you as exes. You're excited however nervous – complete of preference, and on the equal time, weary of what may possibly get up. And rightfully so, because this is pretty a important part of the getting decrease lower back collectively manner and must be dealt with with tact.

If you're going out together together with your ex-woman friend tonight, within the following week, in a few days, or fast, proper here are six do's and don'ts to make sure you are making the most from your first encounter:

Do's

1.Maintain a lighthearted temper in the route of the assembly – Nobody enjoys being in uncomfortable conditions. And this assembly along side your ex is probable to be exactly that: awkward and uneasy, particularly in case you haven't visible every one-of-a-kind in some time. But however this, you can turn subjects round with the resource of retaining it light. Crack a few jokes and make her smile. Make this a fun come upon and more will speedy follow – that's a reality!

2.Contain your excitement – It's natural to be overflowing with excitement in case you've been aside for a while. However, keep your enthusiasm in take a look at. The final thing you need is to provide her the effect that you've been eagerly looking beforehand to this assembly to manifest. Be glad to be along facet her, show it, however don't overdo it. Sometimes men don't apprehend that women should become a tad bit uncomfortable if guys get too excited to appearance them. Weird, you say? It's just a female issue.

3.Keep the meeting brief – If the whole lot's going in accordance to plan, you're finding yourselves wrapped up in thrilling conversations. However, don't make the mistake of dragging out this date prolonged sufficient till you run out of things to talk about and he or she tells you it's time to transport. Keep the momentum going until the time even as the conversation reaches its top, and then, lessen it short. You want to transport away her with something to look in advance to inside the event that she concurs to move on a 2d date.

Don'ts

1.Don't pass there looking like a teach ruin – Going through a cut up can take its toll on every your physical and highbrow state. However, that's no longer an excuse for you to expose up searching like a misplaced stray canine. When displaying as heaps as a assembly together with your ex, by means of the usage of all technique try and restore yourself. Put on some glowing clothes – new ones, if you need – dab on some cologne, and actually generally seem like a higher you. You don't want her to assume the cut up become the right choice, do you?

2.Don't carry up the connection unless she does – Out of all of the do's and don'ts, this is probably the maximum vital so pay close to attention to. After the small speak, you'll be tempted to dive deeper into your past problems. It's humorous how speakme for your ex-lady buddy brings up the past. You may additionally furthermore tell your self which you didn't plan to supply up those subjects, however it's inevitable. But, don't be the one to initiate it. Your only 'venture' finally of this come upon is to region each of you in a snug united states in order that those problems can be properly addressed. You need to recognize that citing the beyond is a land mine which you don't want to step on lest you want the whole thing you worked on to explode.

three.Don't count on an excessive amount of from this meeting – It takes time to recover from the hump of a cut up. But placed the poor feelings aside, and begin over. And it's smooth to turn out to be overly positive about this assembly in case your ex has reached out to you. However, if she agreed to go out with you on a date, it doesn't exactly suggest that she's willing to be with you for an extended-term dating. So regardless of the fact that you're out along side her again, arrive with out expectations. Expecting too much will simplest damage you if worse entails worst. Remember women fall internal and out of affection slowly over the years. So gradual it down.

five Things to Bring to Your Date

Reuniting together with your ex is each awkward and exhilarating. You want to allow her understand that you're inquisitive about courting her all once more, but you need to be cautious which you don't appear too keen or determined. The following is a list of ought to-have behaviors at the same time as you're going to appearance your ex for the primary time:

1.Confidence – Cool, calm, gathered self assurance is what you want to first result in your date together with your ex-female friend. This will bypass an extended manner inside the course of creating your ex need you once more. No don't forget what passed off throughout your cut up, you want to exude an air of self-assuredness that we may additionally want to your ex apprehend you're on pinnacle of factors. However, you ought to no longer confuse self guarantee with cockiness. Being too assured may additionally need to lower your possibilities of being taken decrease back due to the fact she has now idea of you as a cocky guy she gladly left inside the lower back of in the past.

2.Humor – Keep the assembly mild. Keep it glad and maintain your ex comfortable. Humor is a amazing ice-breaker, specifically in case you haven't seen every exceptional for some time. You can also additionally even crack a humorous tale about a commonplace friend and simply revel in the instant and the laughter at the side of your ex. Make fantastic there aren't any awkward pauses or lengthy stretches of silence for the duration of it gradual collectively.

3.Conversation – When seeing your ex-female friend, you need to have a pretty pinnacle concept of what to talk approximately. Stay easy. Ask her approximately what's taking area in her life, what her new hobbies are, what she's been as a whole lot as and et cetera. But don't make it appear like you're interrogating her. You don't need to look like a jealous loopy ex-boyfriend. The communication need to be easy-going and simple. And one ultimate mystery to fulfillment: permit your ex do most of the speaking. You recognize how heaps women love to talk, so permit her. But installation some of your inputs so she acquired't expect which you're clearly letting her bypass on and on. Make it a real communication.

4.Fun – The of you want to reminisce about antique times, further to make small communicate approximately what you've been doing in every other's absence. Reliving the a laugh you as quickly as had will plant seeds on your ex-girl pal's head that perhaps she'd like to preserve that fun through courting you once more.

5.Honesty – Your first 'date' with an ex shouldn't consist of any extreme communicate or talk about the break up. However, if she starts offevolved asking how you experience about matters, it's time for nothing however brutal honesty. When we communicate about brutal honesty, this means no shielding once more. Don't keep decrease again for worry of having your emotions damage. But this doesn't supply the right to really accuse her of being the purpose of the split. Tread lightly. If she's come this an extended manner with you, she desires to understand in that you stand. Give honesty and expect the identical aspect in return. When you do get once more along aspect your ex, you'll each be able to construct on a robust basis of accept as genuine with.

How to Get Your Ex-Girlfriend Back – Even if She Doesn't Want to See You

There are loads of strategies you may use to get your ex-female buddy lower back but most of them may at least require her willingness to reply a cellular phone call from you. But what if she would not even want to talk to you? Here are a few topics you may strive:

☐ Let her understand you're though to be had.

Probably the quickest way to make her jealous is for her to find out you're relationship one-of-a-kind ladies. There is, however, a threat that this could backfire on you. Even if she modified into beginning to remorse the lack of you, once she discovers that you're courting yet again, she would possibly anticipate that you're over her and characteristic moved on collectively with your existence. Therefore, make sure that your mutual buddies are aware that you're despite the fact that single. She's exceptional to take a look at this from them.

Use this time far from her to make improvements on your existence. Build up your self belief or examine a new capacity. Women adore sturdy, assured men!

☐ Write her a love letter.

No, not an e mail nor an SMS - a actual, hand-written letter. Now you may certainly get a threat to provide an explanation for the way you experience. In these days of digital conversation, few matters are extra private than a hand-written be conscious. It may additionally seem like an antique style way to try to get your ex lower lower back but it clearly works. Few women can face up to starting a hand-written letter.

Although it is pleasant to vicinity the entirety in your very personal terms, if you have a problem figuring out what to mention, get a few mind from examples on-line. Remember that the appearance of the letter is form of as crucial as its contents. Choose tasteful stationery, positioned it into an identical envelope, use actual sealing wax and send it off.

☐ Keep it upbeat.

When you do get the opportunity to speak to her yet again, maintain the temper completely glad. Don't pour out apologies for all you did wrong, begging her for a assembly or arguing about some detail prompted the ruin-up. She won't need to appearance you in case you act like an emotional smash!

Rather endorse that seeing you yet again can be amusing and might not contain any groveling or bickering. If feasible, attempt to make her chuckle. You'll be getting her to allow her shield down and take away the "bad aftertaste" left with the beneficial useful resource of the smash-up.

If you would actually need to attempt to get once more your ex despite the fact that she won't move returned your calls, be confident that it is able to be performed. Get your mutual friends to allow her apprehend that you're although single and no longer falling aside from grief, then deliver her a word to make contact again. Be tactful typically; a stupid flow should make matters backfire on you.

How to Get Your Ex-Girlfriend Back When She Needs Space

Many guys normally don't know what to do while an ex-female pal goals area. When a break-up has been initiated via the girl, it often has a few thing to do with "looking location". Typically, while a girl says she goals place in a courting, what she certainly manner is that she's no longer satisfied with the connection. This is a cloaked reaction subsequently of a ruin-up, and can in reality be a cover to keep away from speakme up regarding what's certainly taking place.

Unfortunately, in such times the girl regularly has already decided that she now not wants to be with the character however does no longer need to make the effort to offer an cause for to him why.

When a female says she wishes area, she is indicating that some issue is incorrect.

Rather than discussing the troubles with you with a view to clear up them and get the relationship again on the right tune, she might instead walk away. If you're despite the fact that questioning the manner to get your ex-woman friend yet again even after she says that she goals area, it's miles an outstanding signal. It method you're willing to try to make topics work, so there although is wish.

Her request for location is a clean indication that verbal exchange many of the 2 of you is in some way wrong. In order to have any preference of re-kindling the connection, you need to discover a manner in to discover what is bothering her. This will now not be easy, as she has in fact resolved to shut you out for a few reason, but the state of affairs is by no means hopeless. It's a hassle that does have an answer.

The key to re-igniting a dating with an ex who says she desires region is to discover a way of brazenly talking with every specific. Often, a female will use the need for location as a way of indicating that there can be a flaw within the relationship. Although she won't right away open up approximately that flaw, the 2 of you may in the end need to speak approximately it. Start via making cautious guidelines that you nonetheless need to be a part of her life.

Don't be forceful; as an alternative provide companionship and be privy to how she responds. Once you are greater comfortable in your new friendship, grade by grade probe your manner in a bit extra. Place subtle guidelines inside the conversation about how or in which the relationship ought to probably have lengthy past off-song.

She will open up to you while she's equipped. There's no need to pressure or rush topics; definitely allow the verbal exchange waft slowly and evidently, letting her find out her very personal manner to offer an reason for to you what came about. Once the problems are out within the open, you can with any luck in the end be capable of clear up them.

Chapter 7: Strategies to Help Get Your Ex Back

This might also sound antiquated and possibly sexist but this is no longer the purpose. Rather, our purpose is that will help you re-installation your dating together with your ex-wife or ex-lady buddy. Because people are precise to each specific, it's almost impossible to cover each scenario. Therefore, we are going to stick to generalities for now.

While no proper statistics exist, some human beings estimate that round three-quarters of wreck-usaare initiated with the useful resource of women. What's the motive for this? By and massive, women are extra remarkable of exactly what they want in a companion, on the identical time as men are actually content fabric to "have someone there". Strangely sufficient, it's far usually the girl who wants to get decrease decrease lower back collectively

BUT, if this is not the case, she's now not probable to trade her mind.

Understanding this can assist you get your ex lower once more. You are conscious that you have an up-hill warfare to make matters paintings and that your ex is the one who wants to be on top of things. But - right proper here's the important thing: quality allow her FEEL like she's on top of factors.

The first trouble you want to do is depart her by myself - offer her masses of space and time to anticipate topics out on her private. There is a awesome chance that she'll begin to pass over you, but you want to permit her this opportunity to overlook you. If you insist on calling her and not leaving her on my own, she'll keep seeking to be rid of you. You don't want to look that appear, do you? So, in case you want your ex to get again with you, you can need to break all touch. It may not be easy but it is your fantastic bet.

Now which you've lessen ties alongside facet her, you will have masses of loose time on your palms. However, in desire to simply sitting round, try to parent out what went incorrect. Don't just skim the ground. Try digging down deeply to appearance if you could get to the root of the issues responsible for the harm-up. People frequently cite arguing as a common purpose for a smash-up however besides you understand why the ones arguments occurred inside the first area, you're not in all likelihood to paintings subjects out.

Once you have got recognized the issues, the following step is to art work on techniques to clear up them. One element to undergo in mind is that you may best trade your self, no longer all and sundry else. Therefore, if there are any issues that relate for your ex, you want to either forget approximately them, forgive her or mission her about them. (The ultimate is the most difficult of the 3.)

You need to be willing to do something it takes if you want to get lower back collectively together with your ex. These techniques will not constantly be smooth however will be properly really without a doubt really worth on the same time as to get the 2 of you fortuitously returned collectively.

Nurture Your Relationship

Growing a courting is like developing some thing else, it dreams loads of unique, every day attention. This may additionally moreover sound like a tough difficulty to do, however while you like someone it could be a real pride to motive them to satisfied.

So, when you have acquired the love of your existence lower again and made wonderful that subjects are on the right music for a a success dating, it is time to begin operating at the every day grind of a courting. Let's face it, every day isn't always going to be a fantastic one. Whether you have got were given were given a controversy or taken into consideration certainly one of you gets fired from artwork or your dog dies, life takes area. And healthful relationships are about taking walks through the hardships and always being there for every splendid. It is normally less complex to get through the hard days while you take the time to have a a hit dating each day.

Check out those thoughts for preserving topics glowing and nurturing your dating every day – now not definitely on your anniversary or Valentine's Day.

Have Date Nights

Set aside a night time minimum as fast as each week to spend time collectively. You do no longer even want to head away the residence if you do now not need to, however flip your telephones off and ship roommates or others who stay with you out for the night time if you are staying in. This is mainly vital when you have children. You might also find out it less tough to head away the house for date nights. It in reality isn't always about what you do so long as you spend time collectively. Have some particular guidelines about date night discover it not possible to withstand ought to be just the two of you, you want to do some component that promotes verbal exchange (not go to a film). Whatever suggestions be truly right for you, make certain which you find time to your courting every week.

Be Unexpectedly Sweet

Doing or pronouncing matters which might be candy permit you to nurture your relationship. Every courting is distinctive and has notable wishes. If your ex thinks a few detail you possibly did is amazing, it wishes to be particular. Whether your ex likes your appreciation or affection, discover what makes them feel cherished, rinse, recycle and repeat. Boost their egos (anyone likes it) and provide real compliments to them on every occasion feasible. The great way to do this is through being unpredictable. Never look ahead to the proper time or for them to ask you ways they look. Tell them that they look incredible or seize them at the equal time as their protect is down – after they enjoy lousy, inform them how beautiful they look. Make them revel in unique.

Give Hugs And Kisses

Never underestimate the energy of physical contact in a dating. Hugs and kisses are incredible tactics to show affection. Be incredible that you aren't stingy collectively in conjunction with your hugs and kisses and do not anticipate intercourse without a doubt because of the truth you kissed the one that you love passionately. Make sure that they realise that it's miles ok to be spontaneous and loving with out looking ahead to more. Sometimes hugs and kisses need to absolutely be sufficient. Be wonderful to kiss the handiest that you love every hazard you get.

Show Affection

Showing affection is a super way to nurture a relationship. Modestly being affectionate while in public or with others tells the individual you're with that they will be important sufficient which will permit the area comprehend. Do no longer skip overboard with the general public indicates of love, however setting your arm round your full-size different or kissing them on the cheek on the equal time as in public goes an prolonged way closer to making them feel consistent in the relationship.

Do Things Just For Them

Make positive that occasionally you do topics together which can be best for them. You will now not have all of the same interests, this is perfectly everyday, but you may do topics together even if you do no longer each revel in them. If there can be an activity that the only that you love especially enjoys or a restaurant that they love, make certain to spend time with them selflessly doing matters which can be for them. Even in case you do no longer experience the hobby or the meals, attempt to find out pleasure in most effective being with the person you adore and in giving them pleasure. Make all of it about them.

Say Thank You

Showing appreciation for the person you love is particularly crucial in assisting them enjoy cherished. It does no longer don't forget if it is a massive thing or a touch component, ensure to inform them that you apprehend them every day. Try to be precise too. Do now not virtually say, "I respect you". Say, "Thank you plenty for washing the dishes". It is a extraordinary deal much less hard to accept as true with which you are honest when you are unique. And strive to signify what you assert. Being sincere will go an extended manner inside the direction of creating your big different feel preferred.

Say I Love You

Show your vast particular that you love them each risk you get, but don't forget approximately to tell them that you love them too. Make it a dependancy to tell them that you love them. To make it greater extensive for each of you, you may need to provide you with every other way to say I love you that means some thing to each of you. The film Ghost entails mind. In the movie, Patrick Swayze's character does not tell his girl pal "I love you too", he says "Ditto." This includes have splendid which means for her in the film. Making I love you unique will assist it suggest extra to each of you.

Go Back In Time

Okay, no longer literally. Although when you have a time machine, now may be a exceptional time to move lower lower back and keep away from the heartache of the breakup you are trying to restore now. I digress. What I mean via pass yet again in time is to behave like you're a teen all over again. Remember what it come to be want to be in excessive university and in love? You did crazy, stupid, childish things that mortify you truly to undergo in mind. Do some of the ones things once more. Write every one-of-a-type love notes – on paper, on the bathroom mirror, everywhere. Be innovative.

Also, whilst you are for your high-university kick, keep arms everywhere you bypass together and inside the vehicle at the manner there! Go to a movie that neither considered one of you cares approximately seeing, sit down down inside the lower lower back row nor use the lights taking vicinity as your cue to begin making out! The detail is to have a laugh, humble yourself and act like a toddler again!

These guidelines will assist you hold your dating alive and make you keep in mind why you wanted to save it within the first location. They can also make it easier to get through the hard days. Whatever lifestyles throws your manner, having a robust relationship will make it tons less difficult to cope with something.

Chapter 8: Embark On The Re-Attraction Stage

This is a sensitive level that requires your utmost hobby. If you reduce to rubble this degree, you could should start the manner of looking for to get your ex again anew. However, in case you try this right, you can speedy be talking on the aspect of your ex. The re-enchantment stage calls so one can the touch your ex.

Initiate touch

You want to touch your ex in case you intend to get returned collectively along with her. Remember this brilliant applies you probably did the dumping. This isn't the time to send hateful messages reminding them of ways a superb deal they harm you. This is not the time to junk mail their inbox with voice calls or text messages. This isn't always the time to go go into reverse needy and determined. You need to take a while to consider what you want to say in your ex. There are severa methods to contact your ex. These are:

Text message

Texting has showed alternatively powerful for folks who need to get their ex decrease again. Send a simple text in order to make your ex enjoy proper and a good way to supply them treasured information. For instance, if you see a sale and also you recognize your ex enjoys income, you ought to textual content your ex informing them that you noticed the sale sign and remembered how an lousy lot they love sales. End the textual content wishing them a extraordinary day. Do not tell your ex to text you lower decrease returned. Calling

Calling calls for added attempt than texting. This is due to the fact your ex may be succesful to tell what you feel from the sound of your voice. You want to be calm and accrued if you intend to call your ex.

A letter or e-mail

Instead of texting or messaging, you could ship your ex a letter. Use the equal precept you may use in case you have been texting or messaging. Make your letter brief and non-intrusive. Do now not start explaining your self or speakme about your relationship. Keep it smooth and treasured.

You need to be careful the way you address your ex. Do no longer use the 'domestic dog names' you usually used even as you've got been collectively. You need to chorus from being overly casual. Words like 'babe' and 'sweetie' need to be averted. Just use the man or woman's name. You have to use your discernment to determine out the way to proceed via how your ex responds to you. If you don't positioned your ex immediate, they may greater than probable name or textual content you lower decrease lower back.

Set up a date

The time period date in this situation refers to an day journey or an hobby you want to ask your ex to revel in with you that might probably prevent with a successful cease inside the mattress room or anywhere for that recall. Decide in advance a form of activity you found you and your ex will every revel in. The hobby have to be 'neutral' enough to make your date sense cushty. Make high nice you:

Refrain from using the 'date' phrase

You need to be cautious along aspect your phrases as you communicate together with your ex approximately doing some thing together. The word 'date' will activate pink flags as your ex friends it with unique actions you in all likelihood did on the equal time as you had been courting. Do now not try and recreate different outings you and your ex can also have skilled and do no longer are looking for advice from former outings.

Do now not flirt with others

Do now not make the error of flirting with others in a faulty try and make your ex jealous. Flirting has in no way been particular for relationships. In fact, it's regularly stated as one of the reasons for fights in relationships. If you flirt with others, your ex will partner that with horrible feelings and shun your attempts to get closer.

Be attentive without overdoing it

During the 'date', you need to be attentive on your ex with out crowding her. Include and Engage your ex inside the conversation with out putting them instant.

The cause of your ride is to re-introduce your ex to all the topics that attracted them to you within the first area. As your ex sees you, she is probably able to associate you with appropriate instances and extremely good memories. After a a fulfillment date, you need to be cautious no longer to act too keen to set up for another one. Always bypass for the kiss at the forestall of a date, if she does not kiss you lower lower back, don't act butt damage however smile and preserve it moving. It may be too soon for her, genuinely have the mindset that you could get it next time. Wait every week and time desk your subsequent date.

Rebuild your dating

As can be seen, getting decrease lower lower back collectively together with your ex isn't always an impossible undertaking. It may be completed if you placed inside the effort. However, you want to guard toward being overconfident when you do get returned collectively. If you broke up as quickly as, you can cut up again as long as you've got unresolved problems. You want to work on the ones troubles that added approximately the break up. You additionally want to rebuild your dating for it to grow to be stronger. You have to:

Deal with internal and out of doors pressures

Relationships face both internal and outside pressures. Your very own insecurities may moreover cause troubles on your courting. Your friends and families may moreover make your relationship difficult. You want to artwork on yourself and set barriers in phrases of your courting. Deal with issues in preference to sweeping them underneath the mat.

Cultivate intimacy

Intimacy in relationships can be cultivated by way of way of way of the way you act and what you are announcing on your partner. Emotional intimacy may be very essential due to the fact your accomplice is someone who need to be aware about your thoughts, dreams, needs, wishes, and desires. Physical intimacy is critical as it reassures your companion that you cope with them. The energy of touch want to no longer be ignored. Seemingly innocent touches work well to build intimacy.

Chapter 9: Learn how to talk efficaciously

Learning how to speak effectively will store your courting. A lack of communication frequently breeds battle and misunderstandings. Communication technique citing your perspectives and paying attention to the perspectives of your companion. This need to be executed in a respectful manner. Open your thoughts to precise reviews and don't be afraid to u.S.A. Of the united states your very very own opinion.

Resolve battle

The thriller to successful relationships isn't always avoiding conflict however know-how a way to efficaciously deal with warfare. You need to treatment conflicts in a way so you can go away the every of you feeling happy and respected. Learn the manner to combat honest. Do now not bottle subjects up until they explode. Sit down and talk topics collectively. Keep in thoughts which you are a group. Solving war makes every of you winners.

Keep the passion alive

Don't assume your love lifestyles to burn shiny in case you don't placed some effort into fanning the flames. You and your accomplice want to talk approximately what works, what doesn't and what you could want to encompass for your intercourse existence. Put the focus on 'I' in preference to maintaining a flaw. You can say 'I love it even as you ...' this manner, your associate will feel particular about themselves and want to do greater of that element.

A wholesome relationship gets more potent as time is going through manner of. This is because the two of you have got a observe what works and what does now not paintings. You come to be wiser and learn how to respect every top notch and protect what you have. However, the passage of time does not advocate which you forestall doing the little subjects that offer your courting meaning. There is lots you can do to decorate your dating. Keep sight of the little topics on the identical time as you're making grand gestures. Your dating is critical. Guard it properly.

Chapter 10: The Denial Phase

Denial is the primary of the 5 unique stages of loss and grief. These degrees are greater described in terms of losing someone through dying, but they can also be evident for the duration of breakups—in particular the denial section.

Basically, you're in denial at the same time as you refuse to simply accept the reality, or as a minimum what the fact appears to be. Remember that not all breakups are given a conclusive stop. Most breakups seem to stop with lots of gaping holes with the property you do no longer apprehend. That is wherein the conflict lies.

Getting out of the denial segment is next to no longer feasible in case you ponder upon uncertainty. It is commonplace in a breakup to have numerous belongings you are uncertain of. For instance, you could be unsure if it's miles some thing that you did, if your ex cheated on y0u, if it can have led to every other way, and so on. The motive inside the again of that is that there may be no closure.

Not all people in a breakup is notable sufficient to offer closure for the only being left. This is some different fact that you need to face at the same time as getting out of the denial section. Your price tag out of the denial section and all its uncertainties is finding the closure your self.

Getting Closure

There are critical stuff you have to do if you want to get closure. First, you need to virtually acquire that your unhappiness is real. Reflect on the questions stated inside the preceding section (Understanding your Breakup). Your coronary heart is damaged and your pain is actual. Naturally, you can moreover prolonged for the happier instances you have had together together with your ex. Accept these things now, and soon you will get over them.

Remember that you got your coronary coronary heart damaged because of the fact it is jogging; which means you moreover may also have the ability to heal. Negative feelings are there for a motive, and they may in no way leave in case you keep on ignoring them. Let most of those negativities go together with the float thru you and soon sufficient your mind will pick out to dismiss them subconsciously.

The next aspect you want that lets in you to get closure is to prevent making up thoughts to your head. This is specially difficult in case you suspect that your ex cheated on you. Stick to the proof and accept as proper with in what you apprehend. This is the simplest way so that you can discover the reasons why your ex left.

88

It is also viable that the reasons were apparent and no in addition reinvestigation is needed. For example, your ex in reality cheated on you or is moving to some other u . S . A .. Believe it or now not, these truths are plenty much less hard to just accept.

If now not, you want to find those reasons your self. You can try this by way of manner of remembering your very last conversations collectively together with your ex. Also reflect onconsideration on the matters your ex had informed you in the beyond.

Chapter Activity:

Accepting your terrible emotions is straightforward; but you need a more analytical approach when locating the reasons that added about the breakup. Just do not forget that the entire factor of locating the ones reasons is to acquire the peace of thoughts important for closure. You aren't doing this so you can restore them and get returned collectively in conjunction with your ex!

First, you need to accept all the lousy topics that your ex had stated approximately you. You can also have an obnoxious character, bad personal hygiene, lazy mind-set, and so on. Of route, no longer every one in each of them is always accurate; however you need to take this as an possibility to enhance those topics approximately you. Again, you aren't doing this on your ex. You are doing this to make yourself higher out of self-understand. Go in advance and make a list of these form of terrible traits. For now, hold this list as you may want this for later.

Remember that finding a closure for breakup does not advise you need to positioned a lid on all free ends. Conclude your closure based totally totally on the triumphing evidence. You do no longer need to understand the whole thing that allows you to drift on. Do not waste your effort in searching out all the solutions. Instead, you want to shift your attention on coping with the aftermath of a breakup.

The earlier you start searching earlier, the quicker you forget about what's in the back of you. Having the choice to forget a failed courting and circulate on takes amazing braveness. Whether you want it or now not, it's far the great detail you could do for your self proper now.

Chapter 11: Seeing Ahead

This financial disaster is all approximately:

**Creating new desires in your single existence

**Taking the first step for a higher you

**Cleaning up the mess out of your breakup

Even if you recognize that lifestyles is going on after your breakup, it could be so crippling that you are averted from returning on your antique way of lifestyles. This is every other ordinary response after breakups.

In the previous financial ruin, you are knowledgeable to in reality take delivery of and experience your horrible feelings and permit your thoughts technique them; however for the following couple of hours, you need to disregard them as you attention on the matters for the following day.

Change of Plans

Living a regular life after a breakup also can seem no longer feasible at the start. One purpose of this is the fact that the destiny plans you have got made together together with your ex in the interim are moot. To remedy this, you want to create new plans to your single existence. This is the part of a breakup that might really be thrilling.

Think of it this manner: now which you are free from any emotional obligations, you currently have all of the time within the world to pursue your targets.

Face the information, keeping relationships expenses cash, time and effort. None of these are likely to move once more once they're spent; however now that you are single, you will have these types of sources for your self (except if you are unemployed, in which case you may only have effort and time).

However, you continue to need to clean up the mess. There are a few topics that may be left at the back of by the use of the previous dating. Consider this as your guidance for residing a current-day life.

To start, comply with those clean steps:

1.Delete his/her range—The first actual aspect you want to do is to eliminate your ex's amount from your phonebook. You in all likelihood recollect the precise digits besides, however this can further inhibit the urges of contacting your ex inside the future. This additionally prevents you from'beneath the affect of alcohol texting'your ex or calling him/her even as you are intoxicated.

2.Discard the Gifts and Letters—In making ready your surroundings to your new single life, you need to discard anything that would remind you of your broken relationship. You can throw them away, donate them, burn them, or placed them away someplace you could never see them another time. However, you need to in no manner try to sell them. Selling your ex's affords for you is the worst act of disrespect. Be the higher character and begin your new life thru forgiveness.

3.Avoid Mutual Friends– Unless they may be toward you than your ex, you have to avoid all contact at the side of your mutual pals. This will save you having awkward conversations and being reminded of your ex in case they convey up the problem. Just take have a examine that this is handiest brief. A a part of your new unmarried lifestyles consists of reigniting your social existence, but you do now not need this right now.

4.Un-buddy and Un-comply with your Ex–
'Stalking'an ex's profile is a not unusual dependancy of pretty a few people. This is probably the worst thing you may do to your self right now. It can be tough to definitely take delivery of, however the unmarried lifestyles of your ex is now not your difficulty. Also don't worry approximately acting inclined at the equal time as you do this. Remember that it constantly takes excellent energy to do the proper difficulty; and proper now, that is the right aspect to do.

five.Delete the Photos–What is the detail of removing your social media connections together with your ex if you are retaining pics of her or him except? If you just recently broke up, it can be rather painful to take a look at those pix. It might also even dispose of any possibilities of you forgetting about your ex. Make positive to completely delete pics of your courting out of your pc, social media bills, cameras, mobile telephones and exclusive gadgets. You should moreover delete any motion pictures you have made collectively.

6.Change Playlists– A part of transferring on from a breakup includes listening to numerous tracks that might worsen the manner you experience. This isn't always a awful component with the resource of itself. After all, it enables an entire lot of human beings address the manner they revel in. However, it could prevent some human beings from specializing in different subjects. For now, strive creating a happier playlist to get some optimism.

Chapter Activity:

Take test that each one the steps protected in this bankruptcy take time; but the proper issue is it have to maintain you busy. At this aspect, you have to consciousness on getting even busier.

For this financial catastrophe's hobby, you clearly need to set new dreams for yourself. Take advantage of the freedom you won for being newly-single. As a start, endure in mind your plans for the following 30 days. This should come up with sufficient time to do some thing large alongside aspect your lifestyles.

You are absolutely free to pursue your career, studies new pursuits, sleep at your pal's residence, and so forth. Feel unfastened to move for some thing you want. It doesn't even need to be a amazing accomplishment! To offer you with a few thoughts, right proper right here are four subjects you could do within 30 days:

1.Clean up your House—While you're at it, you can moreover want to perform a popular house cleanup. If you stay in a in particular large domestic, you may need to easy a segment of the house in keeping with day. This need to keep you occupied as you put together for the unmarried lifestyles.

2.Get a Haircut–Why not start your new single existence with a new look? Although it may appear ordinary, getting a haircut can in reality fill someone with optimism and motivation. Just recollect that you are doing this to be ok with your self–choose out a wonderful hair stylist!

three.Perform Charity/Public Service–The first-rate way with the intention to counter bad feelings is to fill your self with first-rate ones. Remember that sincerely because of the fact you experience terrible, you don't need to make humans round you revel in terrible as well.

four.Get a Vacation– Sometimes, you in reality want to break out from the whole lot to attain peace of thoughts. Since you've got got 30 days to fill with smooth desires, why now not encompass a weekend of journey? For now, it's miles lots essential if you need to visit an area in which you'll be on my own at the side of your thoughts. This method crowded places at the side of beaches and concern parks aren't any specific. Consider going to countrywide parks, rivers and different places as an opportunity.

As you go about preserving your self busy for 30 days, you can moreover need to record your enjoy on a personal magazine. Each night time time time, attempt to write as a minimum one get admission to on your mag. Basically, all you need to do is to install writing down anything properly well really worth remembering that befell sooner or later of that day. Try to be sincere at the same time as describing your feelings.

After 30 days, evaluation your magazine and word how many huge activities came about. The question is: are you organized for the subsequent 30 days of your life? And the following?

Cleaning up after a breakup and setting dreams for yourself will great put together you in your unmarried life. This transition might be the toughest a part of handling a breakup. The reason for this is because of the reality no matter the truth that your thoughts and surroundings is ready for starting anew, your feelings may additionally moreover nevertheless be hung-over out of your preceding courting.

Expect to feel frequent waves of loneliness and sadness finally of your first few weeks. They may additionally even last for extra than that. As with any important transition in your life, this takes time.

Chapter 12: Letting Time Heal

This financial damage is all about:

**Believing that 'time heals all wounds'

**Simple methods that allows you to skip the time

**Gearing your self for extra productivity

There is simplest a lot you can do in terms of having over a damaged relationship. Just as how common experience is vain in assessing a breakup, finding an highbrow manner of healing your damaged coronary coronary heart is a waste of time. The handiest difficulty you could do after you advantage this point is to permit time do its process.

However, you will be stricken with the occasional sadness cited earlier. These emotions generally rise up at the same time as your mind isn't preoccupied with something else. So the smooth answer is to distract your private mind with small sports.

Preferably, you want to do extra green sports activities to kick start your single existence. However, it may be impractical as a manner to usually be doing some thing green. For now, here is a smooth interest you could do to distract your self:

Breathe

Getting over a failed relationship may be very distressful. Just the slightest memory to pop up on your head can bring an excessive wave of horrible feelings. This is why it's miles critical which will lessen all contacts and get rid of whatever that can remind you of the past; but some thing you do, fine time can erase the matters in your mind.

Performing respiratory carrying events is a brilliant manner as a manner to distract your self in the direction of traumatic times. It additionally eliminates carbon dioxide, that could be a toxin expelled through your lungs. Breathing is also a brilliant characteristic of your body to preserve your other organs wholesome.

To begin a clean breathing exercising, take a look at those steps:

Step 1: Start collectively along with your natural respiratory

Notice the manner you unconsciously breathe this very 2nd. That is your natural respiratory pattern. Feel the air bypass thru your nostrils and into your chest as you inhale. Then, be conscious the air rush out thru your nostrils as you exhale.

Step 2: Breathe in your belly

In this subsequent step, you want to magnify the manner you breathe via growing your stomach as you inhale. Notice how your stomach muscle corporations tighten as you breathe. Still, you have to be exhaling via your nostrils. From this step on, exercising preserving the air as you inhale for as a minimum three seconds. Repeat 5 instances.

Step 3: Breathe for your chest

Next, you need to awareness your breathing in your chest. As you inhale, you need to take a look at your head bring a chunk as your chest muscle organizations tighten. In this step, you may start to feel a piece lightheaded. This takes vicinity in case you are breathing too rapid or too sluggish. If this takes location, revert again to your herbal respiratory and comply with the sample consequently. Repeat five instances.

Step 4: Breathe out via your mouth

For this step, you could both breathe to your stomach or in your chest. The critical problem is to exhale through your mouth whilst growing a loud sound. As you maintain the air to your stomach or chest, try and curl up your feelings into a ball and expel it out out of your mouth. Repeat for as masses as you need in advance than returning again to your herbal respiratory pattern.

Shifting your popularity into your respiratory is an first rate method of distracting your thoughts and doing something healthy on the identical time. You may additionally feel a touch emotional especially at the fourth step. However, the feelings are greater on the 'calming' facet in place of being painful.

Physical Exercises

One of the incredible methods to deal with breakups is to use them as motivation. It is an infinitely better way to spend time instead of locking your self to your condo and doing no longer anything.

Another advantage of bodily physical games close to handling breakups is the truth that they help your body produce endorphins, that is appeared as one of the frame's 'happy hormones'.

A lot of human beings also accomplice getting into higher shape as a clean indication of development in terms of coping with a breakup. This is truely proper, for the motive that it could additionally be visible as making ready yourself for the following one. It may not be that point however, but it's miles in no way too early.

Remember which you don't constantly want to have weight troubles earlier than you start annoying approximately your health. As a begin, you can installation an exercising/exercising recurring for the following 30 days. Your sports activities do not even need to have a particular diploma of depth. Simple cardio carrying sports together with on foot, cycling, or strolling will clearly be useful for you.

Chapter 13: Focusing to your Career/Studies

By now, you need to have cleared your thoughts enough to recognize what's virtually vital on your existence – your hobby or your research.

The norm has constantly been to get unique grades and to get an tremendous method. Although the relationship maximum of the two might not be as strong as in advance than, training has been proven through statistical records to have a robust correlation with earnings potential.

Other than your career or research, there may be some different detail this is thru a protracted manner hundreds more important than anything on your existence – your destiny.

Keep in thoughts that your existence and your self as a person is surely as vital and as special as your ex. You understand in the lower again of your head which you deserve higher due to the reality it's far true. It can be too late as a manner to put money into your future collectively, however it's far never too past due to pursue your own dreams.

Chapter Activity:

Expressing your feelings thru creativity is concept to create positivity out of all of the mess. It can flip nearly any horrific scenario into some aspect you can in reality recognize in the end. It is one of the maximum mysterious techniques of lifestyles that proves beauty can exist from deep disappointment.

This financial disaster's hobby is all approximately finding your progressive outlet.

Everyone on this international has this innovative ability. Although it could no longer fit the conventional description of 'creativity', there is often a manner for everybody to provide something that others can apprehend.

Of course, this machine can be masses plenty much less complicated when you have already recognized your man or woman abilities and abilties. If this is the case, then all you need to do is to faucet into this expertise of yours and start growing a few factor.

If you haven't decided your creative outlet but, there are two portions of proper news for you:

1.Everyone is entitled to progressive freedom. As prolonged as you experience doing some thing, no one has the right to pick out you. For instance, in case you experience crafting beadwork, then that is a suitable vicinity to start. Do not be afraid to try a few issue new. Only you may discover your innovative capability yourself.

2.You are extra than able to appreciating yourself. Remember that your innovative outlet doesn't mean you need to be as appropriate as anyone else doing the equal aspect. There isn't always any suitable desired for creativity. What's clearly crucial is that it makes you satisfied.

Another manner of inspiring the creativity in you is through allowing yourself to be soaked in your private daydreams. During idle times alongside facet site visitors, showering, ready in line, and so on, do not be afraid to allow your thoughts float away along side your non-public visualizations. Relax and let them fill you with positivity. This will allow you to make touch collectively with your inner passions and hidden aspirations.

Also, you can no longer be conscious it but having a pipe dream is already a innovative outlet with the useful resource of the usage of itself. It taps into one of the most fantastic innovative research any person can have – the electricity of imagination.

While maintaining your thoughts off the past can be very important in moving on from a breakup, now and again severe feelings can accumulate internal you if the ache is simply too amazing.

Take be aware that the time had to mend a broken coronary coronary heart varies for all people. Not absolutely everyone is as robust as others; meaning not all of us can certainly keep on ignoring their unhappiness.

Every once in a while, it's far right an excellent manner to face the ones feelings and allow all of the power out.

Chapter 14: Why it hurts

This chapter is all about:

**Understanding the mechanics of a damaged coronary coronary heart

**Allowing your self to cry is proper in your coronary heart

**Sadness isn't similar to regret

A damaged coronary coronary coronary heart, much like another human gadget, will now not restore itself if it's far constantly neglected. When it comes to getting over your ex, it's far a horrible mistake for you lie about your damaged coronary coronary heart. It is ok as a way to hide it from extraordinary people, however you need to broadly recognized that it's far actually broken.

The key idea within the back of this is to embody the pain.

Take be aware that your emotional pains are normal responses in your mind. These are emotions that want to be expressed. Just similar to the frame's organic way of restoration a wound, mending a broken heart may be simply as painful.

One manner of expressing your deep pain is to cry when you could now not hold it in.

The Benefits of Crying

Interestingly, crying can definitely be a fulfilling enjoy. It is some thing that most humans do regardless of age. With this in mind, you need to apprehend that crying is not something you need to be embarrassed about.

In phrases of mending a broken coronary coronary coronary heart, crying has the following blessings:

1.Emotional Release – Releasing your terrible emotions through crying prevents you from turning them into rage, anger, or perhaps hate. Believe it or now not, crying is the sincerest manner for all of us to particular their disappointment. There is not another suitable way of expressing horrible emotions aside from this.

2.Stress Relief – Crying is tested to do away with pressure-related pollution inside the frame. Just like how blood is vital to shut a wound, tears are essential to relieve pressure and soothe an aching coronary heart. It is likewise hooked up to flush out adrenocorticotrophic hormones that bring about stress.

three.Cleanses your Eyes – Tears flowing from your eyes carry dust and other substances with them. It moreover protects your eyes from foreign irritants. This is why your eyes feel refreshed after an first rate cry.

4.Mood Improvement – Again, crying really occurs even as the emotional ache is in reality too exquisite. If you permit your self to cry, you also are allowing your frame to flush out those emotions till there isn't always anything left. This is why humans sense plenty higher and rested after crying.

Of direction, too much crying also can be a danger. Excessive crying can prevent you from drowsing at night time time, specializing in daily obligations, and dwelling your existence commonly if ignored of manipulate. Fortunately, you are a whole lot much less likely to experience this if you allow your self to cry as described above. On the opportunity hand, in case you keep on preventing your self from crying or forcibly stop your self at the same time as you cry, you are more likely to revel in immoderate crying.

No Regrets

There are sure times while you're emotionally risky and susceptible that you are feeling the want to position the blame on someone or a few issue. This is most effective a ordinary phase of having over someone. In the prevent, you may blame your self for the breakup. This will ultimately motive pretty some regret.

There is not any particular span of time whilst you may revel in this. It might also additionally furthermore arise each every so often; making it difficult so that it will honestly depart the past behind.

This is the issue in that you want to make clean and receive as genuine with that the breakup is not your fault.

It doesn't depend what the unique cause is at the same time as your ex broke up with you. Whether it is some component she or he didn't like approximately you or some element you in all likelihood did now not do, the simplest thing that brought about the breakup is the truth that your ex gave up.

Remember that no individual within the international receives right into a dating and expects it to be first-rate. This is why if you are making plans to look for the correct associate, you would probable as nicely give up already.

Perfect relationships may also sometimes get up, however they in no way final.

Perfect relationships might also stand up while human beings recognize best the exceptional topics approximately every one in all a type; but as soon as the terrible subjects start to reveal, they stop due to the fact they anticipate everything to be pleasant.

On the opposite hand, relationships very last because of the fact human beings are able to work with their accomplice's imperfections and accept them for the manner they will be. They understand the effort their partner is doing to decorate, however do now not expect them to continuously gain achievement in doing so. And this capability to peer thru every different's imperfections and obtain their obstacles is what makes relationships stand the check of time.

Depending at the importance of your damaged relationship, it could take from weeks to a three hundred and sixty five days in advance than you could in reality recover. Take phrase that irrespective of the truth that the ache may moreover ultimately burn up after some weeks, your feelings in the course of your ex take masses greater time to be without a doubt erased.

Chapter 15: Coming Out of Your Shell

This economic catastrophe is all approximately:

**Becoming social yet again

**Saying no to rebound relationships

**Being an emotionally stronger character

There are techniques for someone to approach a modern breakup:

1.You grow to be greater socially active.

2.You have a propensity to withdraw from your social circles.

However, every attitudes will not be effective in moving on out of your ex. This is due to the fact you aren't being sincere with yourself.

First, being extra socially active implies an mind-set of showing faux indifference. By courting, setting out with greater human beings, or participating in extra social events, you're seeking out other folks who can get your attention and distract you faraway from your put up-breakup feelings.

While this is not a lousy aspect thru itself, overlaying your placed up-breakup emotions with low-first rate socialization will no longer let you get maintain of your right emotions. Remember that recognition is a completely important segment of moving on.

This is why rebound relationships are constantly bad thoughts. First of all, if you count on rebound relationships can help you flow into on, then you definitely definately wouldn't be studying a e-book about a manner to recover from a person. Secondly, rebound relationships will continuously make you experience as when you have settled for a person whom you do now not honestly like. This is why rebound relationships never honestly artwork in supporting a person recover from an ex.

However, if you have employed the thoughts-set of retreating out of your social circles, you'll be denying yourself one of the maximum important things essential for managing heartaches–moral help.

Getting Support

One of the exquisite matters you can have thru difficult instances is a pal who listens to you. Keep in mind that your proper friends are greater than willing to apprehend what you revel in, in particular all through emotional instances. This is why you have to no longer hesitate to tell your closest friends what you truly experience inside.

Having a person else who listens is a blessing; it eliminates the revel in of loneliness and can even offer you with superb socialization while you're emotionally unstable.

Eventually, you'll have t0 reignite your social lifestyles via setting out with handiest your closest pals. During those occasions, do no longer bring up the subject of your beyond relationship. Make it all about you and your friends. Strive to create new satisfied reminiscences with them.

Learning from the Experience

It is a reality that the tremendous component you could do in a horrible experience is to examine from it, this is via way of knowing what makes a dating ultimate (Chapter four), the matters that may be unlikable approximately you (Chapter 1 Activity), and a manner to appearance in advance for your unmarried existence (Chapter 2). Notice that everything you've finished up to now to recover from your breakup is a studying experience.

Consider this revel in as an possibility to supply out the terrific in you. Try to paintings on the listing of horrible matters approximately you. Tap into your cutting-edge shops and discover the satisfactory to your pains. All those will in the end flip you proper right into a better and emotionally stronger individual.

Now is the time in an effort to start moving forward.

Chapter 16: The Beginning

Most oldsters do now not want to be on my own and anyone is searching out their one of a kind half of. It is some trouble typically encoded in a person and all and sundry feels greater or loads a good deal less the need to be with a person. After spending time collectively, being under the protective umbrella of a dating, inside the emotional consolation, consolation and protection area, it isn't always easy to get used to the new state of affairs and switch to special procedures of wondering with the useful resource of manner of getting to know to plot your self, spending the day on my own, and residing great on your personal context. The longer the relationship lasted, the longer it is able to take to get another time in your toes. Unfortunately, there may be no magic advice for this and higher temper will embody time. There is lots of fact inside the vintage pronouncing 'time passes and heals all wounds'. You need to acquire that your mind will flow into strongly spherical her for the following couple of weeks. This duration may be shorter in case you really need to get again to lifestyles. It is regular for us to revel in a notable loss even as we break up, the fear of loneliness, your self-self belief falls at the pinnacle, at the start, the tears of sorrow come to the eyes of their private accord. It can not be stopped; you need to cry if you need to. However, it is surely a totally critical duration that forces us to behave, art work on ourselves and expand. Unfortunately, when we are in a dating, in the emotional consolation sector (we're so appropriate, snug, we do now not need to trade some thing), the feeling of the want to art work on ourselves is lots confined than even as we are on my own. People select antique torn 'slippers', with holes in them, frequently already uncomfortable, than the ones you have got dreamed about but are however unproven. That is why they may be stuck in nicely-installed styles. Change continuously brings with it a experience of ache. People hate being alone so much that they choose mediocrity, even a trashy relationship, so long as they have got a few factors of reference, on the manner to recognise their interest on and get this interest from someone. These days love approach that humans keep immediately to every other ineffectively looking to fill their emptiness and their shortcomings and hunger i.E. Popularity and hobby, the revel in of being critical and so forth. And relationships primarily based on such foundations, even though from the aspect they sometimes appear like love, sometimes 'tough love', now and again 'incredible love', in reality they may be no longer in love in any respect. It is more a agreement of humans to satisfy each great's desires than actual mature love. This revel in can exchange your lifestyles for the higher. You need to undergo yours; perhaps that's what you need on your life now within the mind-set of your complete future lifestyles. You're smarter already. Almost all people in life has to undergo some factor like this.

My global collapsed with a bang

"Understand that every 10 seconds in this globe, what takes region to you is occurring to others"

- El Loco

The cut up may additionally want to have befell , and the news about it is able to hit you right away. I'd omitted the caution signs that the woman had given me throughout my first cut up which I skilled most painfully, because it is not the case that a female makes this form of preference from in some unspecified time in the future to the following. Something want to have been going wrong in the relationship for a long time, however it moreover hit me painfully like a collision with a runaway educate. I took her loads as a right. The feeling of being actually surprised with the beneficial aid of a given occasion suggests how improbable it regarded. We did now not consider the opportunity of its occurrence in any respect, however, all relationships are for a time. It is viable that we might no longer be so greatly surprised if we took a second to maintain in mind the threat of it taking place. Nobody is distracted with the aid of the usage of the truth that it snows in wintry climate due to the fact each person expects it. We have out of area a loved one, however isn't always this kind of loss ordinary in human life?

You aren't the number one to experience this, and in fact not the very last. The purpose is that one hundred, two hundred, even one thousand years in the past, humans had the same issues as we do in recent times! People fell in love, parted, broke their hearts, cheated, met, had been given married, staged weddings, had intercourse, have been jealous, cried, laughed, divorced, raised children, out of place their fortunes, and earned their fortunes. That might be so in precisely a hundred years time. We are the same, first-class the surroundings has changed. Nothing lasts all the time, no longer something in any respect! The matters we end up linked to go back decrease returned and bypass. Each courting is time confined. Because because of the fact while were you imagined to have a problem-free life? Nobody has given you any ensures. As Clint Eastwood stated, "If you want a assure, buy a toaster." Everything changes, not whatever lasts all the time, and every factor continuously changes. The trouble is people suppose a few issue is all the time. 'My boyfriend', 'my lady buddy', 'my husband', 'my associate' - sadly, but they all have been satisfactory loaned to us for a brief term in our lives. Perhaps to investigate some thing and skip on because of the fact each courting is for a time. Each one in every of them! Sooner or later, whether or no longer it ends with the painful demise of 1 or the opportunity character, or comes with demise in vintage age, the partner as the first or the husband. People come and then they will be lengthy lengthy past, and absolutely everyone goes their very very own way, because of the reality it's far lifestyles, and knowledge that, likely it's far going to be less complex for us.

People take too many stuff with consideration and are consequently in no manner ready for adjustments or surprising occasions. Remind yourself that the ones pricey human beings do now not belong to you (unless we are talking about slavery) and are given to you great at this 2nd, no longer for eternity. This is the fact, irrespective of how sturdy your affection for someone is. Enjoy what you have right now as it can be taken from you right away. Sooner or later, every body well-knownshows out approximately it of their lives.

Don't blame her because of the fact some time together is virtually over. We are all couples nice brief...

Severe withdrawal signs and signs and signs

"-Why should I drop my past? Not all of it is awful.

-The beyond is to be dropped no longer because of the fact it is horrible but because it's miles useless."

- Anthony de Mello

She is your heroin that destroys you, even though you love her a lot. You must find sufficient electricity to say, "Enough of this shit" and do it. It is a struggle to go back to a short restoration! Showing the strength of will to move on with our lives at the same time as our mind is trying difficult to get slowed down in the depths of the past is a war. Your thinking, behavior and behavior are designed to preserve your ache from no longer going away. You're lacking the medicine. Dismissing romantic love activates the same mind mechanisms which is probably activated even as addicts withdraw from substances like heroin. You display all of the symptoms and signs and symptoms of dependancy due to the fact what you enjoy is particularly dependancy to the opposite person. You lengthy to get the drug back and revel in it appropriate all over again. As with each addiction, there comes a detail in which get entry to to the drug is denied, then it starts offevolved to harm more than ever. It's like a completely underneath the have an impact on of alcohol guy who thinks everything is fantastic and simply maintains pouring even more alcohol into himself with out understanding it. You are actually like a drug addict going to the supplier "please provide me a dose, I'll perform a little factor so can virtually deliver it to me!" You do not understand what to do. You begged, you cried, you apologized, and possibly you drove to her house and made a entire idiot of your self. Tirelessly you search for the tiniest sign of preference. In the end, the female loses all of her respect within the route of you and does not need to have something to do with you too. Then we are gone, and for her we sincerely cease to exist. So we are capable of strive really whatever to get again the (drug), the sensation of the man or woman we love.

She is now for you, as for Gollum, the One Ring. You ought to loose your self from her truly. You have withdrawal syndromes, and every of her messages, every contact together with her, each take a look at her snap shots is like taking every different dose - in a manner it permits (unpleasant illnesses disappear), but it does now not sincerely heal and the addiction persists.

It's time to take remedy, lessen off any touch and abide with the useful resource of this option and paintings on your self to turn out to be appealing. Put the drug down. For the ones addicted to candies, it's far difficult to fight in the candy keep.

Chapter 17: Master your impulses

"Don't consider everything you trust you studied. Thoughts are surely that, thoughts."

- Buddha

Human nature is perverse. People look at what has become unbelievable for them, and what escapes from them is inaccessible. Then they assume a higher charge of some component. Your ex-companion driven you away, this is why you started out to transport after her. You see her go away and also you try to run after her and save you her. This is your problem when you value too much what you 'lose' with out understanding certainly what you can advantage. You enjoy a loss, and it's far normal to want to hold a kingdom in which you are not on my own. After a while, being with a person will become regular. It's the disappointment, fear, dwindled vanity, the notion that no one is probably placed. You suppose to yourself that you want to fight for her because of the fact you'll lose her all the time. She's lengthy long long past anyway.

"But I love her" – you're pronouncing. Believe me that every folks loved, however through the usage of some abnormal accident, each humans loves them even more after they leave us at the back of, and whilst they come and say they do not want to be with us anymore, abruptly our love reaches its apex. It's the extraordinary reality, isn't it?

Our mind is not this sort of right representative as we think. You truly can't don't forget it. The deer's thoughts tells her to run even as she feels that she may be in hassle, she offers in to feelings, impulses, terrible advisors and runs ... Directly into the street. Many of our behaviors, which inform us a few aspect in our heads, imply that we simplest lengthen our pain, delaying the restoration method, or maybe in the end motive issues with highbrow fitness or alcoholism.

Lots of human beings revel in panicked after extended relationships because of the fact they do not bear in mind what it's far want to be on my own anymore and they may be scared of it. Many human beings derive their experience of price and splendor from being with someone as in case you, as an independent entity, had no raison d'être. Someone who builds vanity in a courting, will become hooked on their partner, loses themselves and junks their accomplice.

What are you going to do now? At this degree you aren't amazing what will seem subsequent. This is everyday. You want to head loopy. As prolonged as you are stricken by emotions, you are panicked and there is not some thing you may do, because the entirety you do now on this us of a will not help you. Emotions play the primary play around in you. You recognize the vintage challenge has already ended, but you are now not sure what to do collectively together with your existence now. Simply wait. A breakup is an indication of improvement which you may mistakenly take into account a sign of failure. Remember that regardless of the truth that you do no longer have a girl pal now, you have got always been, and is probably treasured, unconditionally.

It's difficult to swallow, but I accept it

"Pain is inevitable. Suffering is non-compulsory."

-Haruki Murakami

She should not want to be with you anymore and also you need to be for the reason that. What, are you will be moaning like some woman now? Give me my girl friend once more. Give me returned my toys? You ought to accept that's it's far a residing man or ladies and in case you love this man or woman, you need to want her to be satisfied. But maybe your definition of love is to love this being terrific if it gives you with the drug in the form of intercourse, falling in love, intimacy, and so on. Don't permit yourself to accept the reality that she now wants to supply this drug to someone else or be on my own. It is not her obligation; her obligation is to head in a route that makes her satisfied and appealing to her. We are so egocentric that none human beings bear in mind it that manner.

If you certainly cherished your ex-woman pal, why no longer allow her locate what she dreams, and now not really what you need? It's her. Could or not it is selfishness and no longer love? Huh? If you cherished her, would not you permit her have Happiness with a capital 'H'? To love in order that the need to have a girl isn't inscribed on this love. To love simply so within the meanwhile at the identical time as a female makes a decision to move away, you can lightly say: "if you need it to be happier - pass, and I simply wish you this happiness".

You can't help it. Therefore, you need to neglect about her. If some problem has damaged, there may be no element in fixing it, and for you it's far going to be a miles higher detail to be with someone else who will virtually along with you, love you and admire you for what you're. You meet a female because of the reality you want to offer her happiness, pride, moments of pleasure and unforgettable impressions. If she does not need to, you can not make all people happy. Accepting the reality that the best you want not wishes you is the lowest, the inspiration of releasing yourself from those awful, aching feelings.

What might be greater futile and crazy than the introduction of an internal resistance to some thing that already passed off? When you bang your toe after which fight this pain, the pain appears even worse. But while you hit your self and say fuck it. If it hurts, then it hurts, and that is high-quality! Suddenly it is as even though the pain is going away. Surrender to what is due to the reality the ache because of the lack of a loved one want to be transformed via popularity. Accept what you do not want to just accept. Acceptance does now not mean state of no activity; reputation is actual electricity and adulthood. Learning to simply accept what we cannot alternate it tough sufficient and implementing. Accept your ache, it'll harm plenty less.

When painful recollections come to you, give up to them and gain what's now and what you sense. Don't combat or push them away because of the truth you are in quicksand and preventing will handiest make the pain worse.

How not to transport loopy - the first few weeks

"I should lose myself in movement, lest I wither in despair."

- Alfred Lord Tennyson

Help at domestic. If you have your private residence or condo, there can be generally something to do there, so smooth up, wash the cabinets, sew a button on, iron your shirts, clean and polish your shoes, smooth the home home home windows, smooth the glass within the wall unit simply so there are no stains. Wash the rest room, easy the tiles, the sink from the pinnacle to backside, and easy the floors.

Look via wardrobes for garments which is probably antique or torn out - there might be at the least 2-3 devices. Think about what desires to be steady and attempt to do it; and in case you cannot do it now, reflect onconsideration on the way to do it.

Call buddies you have not seen for a long time. Make an appointment with them. See if you could examine a language so that you can cross someplace in the summer time. Plan something, write down what you want to do, and begin putting it into motion.

Go cycling or fishing. Go for a run or watch a comedy. Meet up together with your friends. Clean up the house. Wash the dishes; just do everything to take your mind off her. Do the whole thing no longer to consider her. Renew neglected and precious contacts or do some issue genuinely extremely good. Stop residing most effective for that piece of ass or you may die miserably. You have free time so loosen up out along side your buddies, play on the console, chat along side your circle of relatives, construct submarine models, discover ways to lessen and sew, take a look at books, smooth aquariums, etc.. Fill up your day so that you do not have time to feel sorry for yourself and mirror in your ex.

When you undergo, you have to face up to the temptation to sit down down and brood over your sadness. A very sensible plan is to update fruitless self-torment with workout. With bodily try, you reduce the weight on the a part of the thoughts wherein reflections and spiritual suffering are located. Another part of the brain directs the muscle attempt just so your pain is broken down and relieved. Physical hobby in this manner triggers the discharge of endorphins, the happiness hormone.

In 3 months time, it will be over. Set your self a time restriction to your head. So you suspect that after 2 weeks things gets better. DON'T DELUDE YOURSELF, as there is probably more shit than now, extra than you believe you studied and further than you could even take into account and further than humans need to ever remember and describe. It can be horrible, keep in mind me. But then pass for a run someplace in location of taking walks lower back to her. Zero writing! Just consciousness on your self and hold attempting. You will harm down more than once, so deliver yourself 3 months to be in a fucked up state.

I recognize, it appears oh good-bye, but you can no longer even have a take a look at it. The first weeks, then the number one 2-three months could be tough. Then it one manner or the other flies, and also you gather yourself collectively, and also you do not touch her in any manner. Exercise persistence, persistence and one extra time staying electricity and of route no touch alongside side her. In just a month or , you will be a totally unique individual. If you discover ways to anticipate proper and do what you need to do, then you will be, - it is assured. Each day works in your advantage. Over time, you may skip again on your reminiscences a good deal much less and lots an awful lot less.

Over time, you slowly come to the element where you find out emotional strength for existence beyond a misplaced relationship. We learn how to love existence and certainly one of a type humans anew, and all attention isn't directed handiest to what we've got out of vicinity. Many human beings have a tough time with this challenge. We are afraid that we are killing the memory of a out of vicinity individual with the useful resource of reading to love lifestyles or unique people anew. Above all, deliver yourself time. Treat it as if it's far not for your existence, as though something particular happened to you, however you understand that a few aspect even higher will rise up to you. Work on your self! Be patient especially, and

outcomes will ultimately come.

A lot of human beings say that while you sleep with some one-of-a-kind ladies, that feeling wears off, however I recognise it is too early for you and you do not revel in as much because it. You nonetheless deliver indicators to those round you which you are sad, even if you are not privy to it. You probably have a hint loathing of girls now - you excellent care approximately this one, and you do not need to pay attention

149

about any other, let alone some relationship. Take care of various matters. If it hurts, so be it. Wait a 2d because of the reality you need this time.

Do no longer pressure yourself to look for a girl now, it's going to kill you. Don't get into new relationships. Meet human beings, visit the gymnasium, play tennis or some thing. If you do now not wait, you may no longer go through, and you could only eliminate the ache that is to come decrease lower back. You need to undergo yours and go through what you want to. Do now not are searching for comfort the least bit prices. Everything has its private rhythm.

Nutrition: How to manual mood and highbrow health

You should realize that weight loss program, the scenario of our intestines and what we offer to our frame is largely answerable for our well-being. You ought to relieve your tense gadget and brain, after the ones last probably sleepless nights and robust pressure which continuously saved you agency. If you don't address your thoughts and body which you acquired't have the energy of mind to do the paintings that need to be accomplished to get better after painful breakup.

•Junk food=depression. Avoid food that might make your overwhelming feeling of disappointment worse. You must avoid trash, processed food for as a minimum for the closest future. By the way, now may be additionally the great time to alternate your eating conduct to greater healthful ones, the ones so you can serve you higher. Avoid sugar, synthetic sweeteners, alcohol, hydrogenated oils, rapid meals, trans fats, processed food, soy souce. But do now not allow yourself to go hungry, due to the fact that's while the worst moods get us. Good amazing diet regime: Healthy fats like extra virgin olive oil bloodless pressed. Fatty fish rich in Omega-3s which incorporates salmon, herring, mackerel, anchovies, sardines, tuna. Nuts which encompass walnuts, almonds, cashews, peanuts. Avocados. Fresh greens and stop end result. If you want to be without a doubt alive, you need to have the proper gasoline.

•Vitamin B-complex. Our concerned tool is strongly inspired through each element of strain and want vitamins from organization B. Supplement for a length of min. 2 months.

•Ashwagandha. Its a totally precise plant that has been used for masses of years, it has super tension and stress decreasing residences for the nervous device. It has an antidepressant effect. It's used in states of exhaustion, anxiety, tension. That's why you may furthermore want Ashwagandha that lets in you to assist your organism adapt to disturbing conditions, emotional screw ups and severa poisonous relationships. It's now not addictive and has no factor outcomes. It's without a doubt natural. Usually one or pills an afternoon is sufficient to revel in the distinction after some time.

•Vitamine D3 (solar publicity). Vitamin D is needed for mind improvement and characteristic. Vitamine D3 5000 IU (units) an afternoon.

•Probiotic complement. Probiotics are live suitable bacteria that provide fitness benefits normally by means of using way of enhancing or restoring the gut plants. Gut microbiota's effect on intellectual fitness. The gut and brain are connected. These organs are related each physical and biochemically in a number of specific strategies. Basically, your intestine microbes can help your body produce greater serotonin and extraordinary authentic chemical substances that impact your mind.

•Cold-water therapy. Ice baths can appreciably reduce your stress, tension, and despair. There is a lot of data about the advantages of bloodless baths/showers. Some medical doctors do not forget that swimming in bloodless water has healing effects on the human psyche. Ever since the ancient instances, they had been preferred for their limitless fitness advantages. Cold water remedy has a excellent effect on bodily and intellectual health. It soothes melancholy and improves your mood. It lowers strain stages. Icy baths offer us a more self notion and boom of religion in our non-public talents, as it's miles related to overcoming fear. Look online for the Wim Hoff Method (The Ice Man) it permit you to lots! Start with regular bloodless showers each day for 30 days. At the begin you could change bloodless and heat water. You will see how lots higher you'll enjoy physical and emotionally.

Chapter 18: Wipe your nose

"Self Pity -- I in no way located a wild problem sorry for itself. A hen will fall frozen useless from a bough, with out ever having felt sorry for itself."

- D.H. Lawrence'a

You can cry at domestic. You can howl and I apprehend you may, particularly at the start, but on the street you can recreation a smile in your face. You are ironed, washed, shaved and straightened up. In three months time, it will in all likelihood be over. Set yourself a time and exercising your muscle agencies. However, protect your self at the gym, due to the fact in case your head is distracted, you could harm some aspect. Exercise and do it hundreds (however with commonplace experience!) In three months you could effects lose or gain 6 or 7 kg to your muscle mass. I do now not recognize whilst you're studying this, in all likelihood it's far nonetheless wintry weather now, spring will begin in March and you may be equipped for something new.

Get out to the people. Sit down and loosen up somewhere. If you ever favored to, buy some first-class footwear or a shirt. Relax and get a rubdown. Set your self a reduce-off date to your mind after which you can start to characteristic typically. Do no longer behave as in case you are „the most effective who suffered at the flow", as an photograph of suffering of a substantial variety. Do you think that if she noticed you currently inside the country you are, it'll make an influence on her? You must give her some different excuse to run far from you even similarly. Be yourself, without a doubt the modern day you, and ideally search for some trouble cool and most importantly, some thing new.

Let out all of your emotions, do not keep a few thing inner. If you need, write to a relied on friend. Throw insults, piss your self off, cry, howl, but in no manner do it on the street. In the road, you need to be smiling and upright, together with your head held excessive. Be shaved, combed, and normally put on clean garments. Force yourself to grin earlier than going out anywhere. Do it inside the the front of the mirror, each time you depart the house. Biggest mistakes at the equal time as breaking-up

"The number one purpose (of suffering) is innate lack of know-how and the ensuing choice for topics to be apart from they may be"

- The Tibetan Book of Dreams

Real lifestyles is not much like the simplest in american movies or Disney fairy memories. These films or animations commonly stop properly and the efforts of the heroes are rewarded with happy endings. Unfortunately, this isn't the case in lifestyles. You ought to behave differently than in the films and not observe their example.

•Asking for pass once more and a second threat. Nothing is greater pathetic in the eyes of a female, then even as a person begs for forgiveness. In order to break-up a female has to have lots aversion in the direction of a man, to promote off him and no longer have a responsible moral sense approximately it. Otherwise, she could cry every night, due to the truth she's a lady and ladies are emotional beings. She has to gather enough self notion not to have any doubts about the damage-up or getting back together. With your request, you positioned your self within the role of an applicant for some detail, you display this via way of the "plead" method whilst you realize that you are (at the least on your opinion) inferior, so that you attempt, plead due to the reality you enjoy that you'll in no manner get something better...So you run with flora and so on. Apologizing with plant life must have exactly the same stop cease result proper right here as loads of diverse situations, so the opportunity of the one intended. All of our pathetic moans are absolutely omitted. We handiest verify to her that we aren't without a doubt what she - a girl - wishes. How are we able to be? By breaking our dignity, we go through even greater, we deprive ourselves of our personal apprehend, even as getting actually nothing. Absolutely now not something. You are begging for emotions and women NEVER forgive that.

•Let's stay pals - allow's be sincere, you don't need to be her buddy, you want to be her man. You don't need anymore pals. An undoubted advantage of such "friendship" is the pain comfort it offers.

It's like a shape of morphine which eases the ache of a damage-up. However, there may be a very uncomfortable detail right here. There is no dating. You despite the fact that love her, however you could't kiss or have sex collectively together with her and you don't have the possibility of forgetting about her. The woman is constantly for your mind. And you persevere in lethargy for some time, till a trendy character whom she begins to fulfill up with appears, and also you stand with not anything due to the fact all this time you weren't doing whatever, just equipped and living in desire that perhaps if you persevere she can change her mind. This isn't the manner! Very regularly an ex is retaining a former ex because he's a exquisite device of validation - not some thing caresses an ego quite like an ex who can't come to terms with the lack of you. You need to continually forget approximately it, you don't offer a shit about her and that's that. Keep your honour, the doll would possibly not need you - too horrible, bye, find out your self a few homies to hang around with in preference to gambling a lady buddy for her.

Your thoughts-set

Adulescentia est tempus discendi, sed nulla aetas sera est advert discendum.

Eng. "Your teens is the time for reading, but no age is surely too antique for that."

If you cry due to the fact she has left you, how are you going to provide for her own family? You cry at the same time as you do now not have enough coins for some detail? You are to be much like the leader of the tribe! A disaster is drawing close; you take a spear and cross seeking to maintain her stable, that her youngsters live in abundance, that they do not lack some thing. After all, girls want help, they want right genes in someone. Do you determined a crying dude will supply her that? A guy who can not deal with adversities? And what's going to occur at the same time as you get fired from your procedure? Will you spoil down? Why does she need someone like that? A girl needs someone to beneficial resource her. She's supposed to take care of the residence, and you need to art work your ass off and hunt for her and your children. Well Snap out of it. It's happened, she has lengthy gone. The worst element is to panic and display her your conduct which you are a loser. DO NOT CRY! Don't beg, do no longer ask, because it won't do any correct and do not make an apology to her. Do you need to apologize to her for breaking apart with you? Logical arguments do now not art work on her. It is inspired by way of the use of herbal instinct and feelings. Show her that you are a flesh-and-blood man in the end; take it together with your head held excessive. During the conversation, if she tells you that she desires to go away, appreciate that, and if you can smile, then do it. Say that her choice is difficult to swallow, however you respect it and acquire it, and want her the high-quality, and regardless of how strongly internal you're tearing your emotions, whilst you're on my own, you could cry as lots as you need if it permits, but not in the front of her. If you are already humiliated and weakened, as I begged and requested for your time, then if it grow to be some days within the beyond, write that you care, but you recognize her choices, and so on. From now on, the hard avenue begins offevolved. The high-quality you could do is live silent, ruin the contact in reality, and if you see each different cope with her like a chum, without any sensitivity. If she calls, say you are busy. This damage-up will provide you with a kick, but that kick is your choice for exchange. Maybe manner to this you will determine to open a enterprise, learn how to play a brand new tool, get inquisitive about martial arts or cope with your appearance. (That's what you favored!)

During this time, she can be able to find out a person, the so-called Comforter. The worst aspect you could do is beat him up or throw him down or threaten him if you met her somewhere with a few guy. Greet her in a polite way, be confident, and certainly put together yourself mentally. When you meet someplace at a celebration, come and alternate some sentences and feature a outstanding time, do no longer examine her. Take care of different girls, now not for display, however because of the reality you truly experience love it, and you likely did no longer come right here for her ultimately, but to have a laugh. You do now not need to show some aspect to her. She would not interest you anymore, and do now not show some thing to her, your ex, buddies or her parents. Do the entirety for your self. Why perform a little component for show, there can be no need to do it, and there are particular interesting well-knownshows which are virtually properly really worth spending time and electricity on. You want to with the aid of a few approach 'play lower back' on for this? Why? Would someone do this? Come on, inform me? Doing some issue to get another time at your

ex is initially a evidence that she stays bothering you, secondly a display of susceptible component, and thirdly, a proof that in spite of the truth which you've were given turn out to be a more than not unusual seducer, you still have now not determined something new considering you've got were given were given time to struggle thru the dirt of the beyond like a bit little one in a puddle, I anticipate it is time to enlarge up ...

The woman does not need a 2nd 'pussy' in her environment. She clearly desires a person, a man, a rock. Will you ease your pain thru behaving in a manner unworthy of a person?

Gulf idea

The scenario of being dumped through a girl has plenty to do with popularity on a gulf. An abyss office work among the 2 of you, and you could't conquer it. It simply is. The gulf is her choice. At this thing, it's now not viable to jump over the space. She produced it, and he or she or he or he need to begin to regret doing so. The distinction some of the two of you is that she is status with her back to the chasm, at the identical time as you face it and check her. What do you suspect, how will a leap beforehand prevent? When you start on foot to her, what will arise to you? The most effective choice is to fall into the abyss. You take one small step and fall. Then for her and for your self you are for all time misplaced. Possibly, out of remorse she makes a choice to throw you a rope and gets you out. However, as quickly as she judges which you have recovered she might be able to throw you lower back into the chasm and you will be back inside the equal vicinity. The moral of this is that steppin in the course of her, chasing her, bothering her simplest makes subjects worse. You can shout to her, the space isn't massive sufficient for her now not to pay attention you. The trouble is that she doesn't need to pay attention you. Besides, on the same time as she is dealing with faraway from the gulf, she isn't looking yet again, she will't see you, however she can though pay attention, for her it's a signal which you are but near and every time she choses she can be in a position to turn to peer you, you, an abandoned terrible mutt.

So what can be carried out in this example? There isn't any notable way, you want to turn your again at the gulf, don't look down, do no longer don't forget how to triumph over it. On her element she will quick discover many powerful factors. Don't permit for your component to be an area of unhappiness and remorse. Because on one hand you have got got a gulf, but on the possibility a big vicinity. It's time to move earlier, stroll faraway from the chasm with assured steps. Move ahead. Arrange your self over. I assure that there are masses of splendid women, friends and opportunities in your side. Your detail has many pluses, you could installation some time but you need, start going to the health club. Really, you could carry out a little thing! And by no means, ever look decrease returned. Go right now ahead, as some distance as viable. Zero searching over your shoulder, actually beforehand.

At some point, your ex will come to the gulf out of hobby, ultimately she can be inquisitive about what you are doing, the way you're managing subjects, perhaps she'll leave out you. She last found you even as she created the chasm and also you cried, apologized. How amazed will she be whilst you're now not there. If that's no longer sufficient, she received't also be able to see you on the horizon.

Now there are three alternatives:

She will start to shout loudly, calling you over to the gulf. If you return going for walks right away she might be able to suppose that you're nevertheless waiting simply nicely tucked away somewhere. And she can be capable of turn once more. And you, in which will you be? Over the chasm over again. That's why it's nicely without a doubt worth it to dismiss her screams. Go even similarly in order now not to pay hobby them.

The 2nd option is that this. She includes the gulf, she begins offevolved to shout, but she will see that the scenario is hopeless, that you are lengthy lengthy past, you arranged your lifestyles, you're dealing with, you've changed. She will then flow into crazy, however you can't come once more to the gulf under any situations. Live your lifestyles. She created the distance so she has to consider the way to dance it. And even though it's a one hundred-metre lengthy gulf, if she cares approximately you she will soar it with none problems, she may be capable of find out a way. Then she can be capable of want to pressure her manner through your aspect and you could slowly allow her returned into your international, wherein your rules be triumphant. This is your area, wherein you are a completely unique guy, hard, durable, richer in opinions and confident. Then you will yourself recognize, in case you need to allow her decrease back into your international, or go with the flow for a walk collectively with her inside the path of the abyss, grasp her via way of the collar and ship her flying decrease returned to her side with one kick, developing an terrific more gulf.

The 1/three preference isn't always very impressive. She never includes the chasm. She wasn't properly really worth of you.

No Contact

She should now not exist to you. The quicker you recognize this the higher. Any interest in what she is doing is risky on your mood. No touch. No fucking birthday's, no grandpa's loss of life or brother's being pregnant - no cause. Do I offer my fucking condolences to my "former ex"? No!!! Because I don't provide a fuck about her. I in reality don't care approximately her. You ought to recognize 0 touch. It's the handiest feasible way out for you and your highbrow fitness. She can't see you, and you cannot see her. It can be a lot less difficult to make changes. Believe me. The heaps a lot much less contact, the calmer the mind and soul. Are you still trying to get her again? Then forestall! It's the first rate, and sometimes the ONLY desire. The a great deal less contact the higher. Let go - you'll be more healthy.

The reality that you will be seeing every exceptional - is NOT suitable. Even thru Facebook. Today, it is rather easy to spy on someone. We have get right of access to to the net, google, fb or different structures that may provide us with pretty some statistics within the form of textual content, photographs or video. But, you want to understand that every second devoted to tracking your ex on the internet, checking how she is reasons you to feed your dependancy and deepens the pain you experience. Do you need to break the dependancy in your ex? Then you have to get rid of all lines of the addictive substance. One have a study her new facebook photograph, pics from events, pics of her with a few new guy can ruin you all over again for a few different few days or a whole week. Deselect your ex so that you don't look at her. Peeking at her snap shots, assembly collectively along with her - although it brings you brief alleviation, it's like taking a painkiller for a tooth that desires to be pulled out. Sooner or later the pain will come back.

Do you understand what zero is? Not 2%, no longer five% or fucking birthday/Christmas Eve desires. So you need to quit your addiction, however you still have her cellular phone huge variety, you follow her on fb and instagram, and also you maintain your shared pics to your telephone? What the hell do you need that for? You don't need her huge variety. You assume to your self "I received't delete her quantity due to the fact if she calls me I received't realize who's texting/calling me"- Do you've got the range for your number one college janitor in your phone too? Because you want to recognize that it's him at the equal time as he calls? No! You don't want to delete her from your facebook buddies because of the reality that's infantile, you placed your profile up so that you forestall obsessing her. You can set your instagram up so that you nevertheless take a look at her, however her hobby (posts, photographs, memories) aren't displayed for you.

"But I'd want to apprehend who she's assembly with and what she's doing"- It received't do you any well! She can also even stand on her head and also you won't care…Get it? You need to permit the wound heal, however if you keep reopening it, peeking, sprinkling it with salt, there may be no way it will get better.

You have 2 choices:

•You do no longer touch her, the chick comes again to you crying because you aren't chasing her - you win.

•You do not contact her, the chick doesn't come, you heal faster - you win.

In each situations - YOU WIN

If you hold in touch you're fucked; melancholy, alcohol, the shortage of capability to speak to a trendy girl, typically fucked.

Just like a soldier on the wall

"Don't be embarrassed approximately trying help. You have a duty to meet just like a soldier at the wall of conflict. So what in case you are injured and may't climb up without some different soldier's assist?"

— Marcus Aurelius, Meditations, 7.7

The centre of the thoughts that is responsible for physical pain is the identical one this is activated when we're rejected, because of this rejection will harm us truly as an entire lot as a damaged leg or physical ache. As with the physical situation, we go to the physician to address the wound, and right proper here we look for help from others. You are critically injured and you want assist from unique soldiers. As men, we adore to anticipate we are able to cope with it all on our own. Do no longer close yourself in your personal pain. Some human beings prefer to revel in the alone and it could art work for them. However, when you have such want to get assist from own family and pals, however you're afraid that they will no longer understand you, in all likelihood they may laugh it off; they'll now not want to pay attention to it, in any other case you do not need to confess that it hurts you and you're ashamed, and so on., then try to get this manual, find out it, if no longer right right here, then with someone else. If a person makes amusing of it, it manner that he is not a real guy and has by no means expert it in his life. Now you want to undergo it at the manner to grow to be this form of man. It's quality if you have such an opportunity so that it will start residing in an surroundings of a loving own family (dad and mom, siblings, cousins, and so forth.) and buddies, close to buddies, and girl friends, or professional help. Don't assume its unmanly to invite for resource. You'll get out of this faster.

Your pal tells you to satisfy with him, or bypass somewhere with him or other pals, and you say, "I'm now not feeling nicely, I'm now not in shape, I opt to stay at home." What need to you do then? You ought to go out, then you can say later which you had a wonderful time, but while you acquire home you began out to undergo in thoughts her all over again, but for those few hours your thoughts became distracted and it helped you. Try to renew or rediscover the lifestyles you had before your relationship. You need to reactivate your new life as a unmarried. Before you broke up, you have been unmarried and possibly it modified into a few years ago, however you have been single and one manner or the alternative you've got got been doing well. You can be k now, and you need to like being single for some time and stand to your very non-public toes. You will understand that you can have an notable lifestyles being single, even if you do not want to be single right now.

You do not need to address the entirety yourself, if you want assist my friend, in reality ask. The extra help you could get, the quicker you'll get better.

Chapter 19: The cause she broke up

The call adjustments but the issues stay the equal because they're inner us. That is why it's so vital to delve into yourself once in a while, no longer to break out from yourself to the TV, internet, amusement, activities, alcohol, however to do not forget yourself. The place to begin want to be a actual, entire knowledge of the mistakes that have been made, and the faults that must be dealt with. It is ready being absolutely aware of her shortcomings, however it's miles within the maximum critical the attention of your private faults that permits you to surely understand your self. There are numerous women round, and I do not absolve her from something, but most of all, not seeing fault for your issue for the same errors dedicated again and again all over again will suggest that there be no positives from breakups and subsequent relationships. It is in fact worth taking a have a have a look at why it's far going on this manner and not in a exclusive manner, and it's miles rattling difficult to get an affordable view on the identical time as our emotions are raging. Then we're very susceptible to all tips, and the patch on the burning wound in the shape of a way to the 'why?' question becomes a valuable commodity. So a notable deal that we are able to locate the answer anywhere and healthy every solution, due to the reality each seems to healthful. Sometimes, in fact, It's no longer each person's fault, and no individual is sincerely accountable, and the one who first realizes that falling in love is one detail and mature love is a few different then goes away. Nurturing the hatred of the 'recommend whinge' isn't always the only approach. Therefore, it's far sincerely lots much less tough to say "I fucked it up!", however, alternatively, you need to now not strain your self to search for remarkable guilt and carrying sackcloth. Of route, if you do no longer draw any conclusions from the mistakes you made inside the previous dating; if after studying what you have been, you do not diagnose what you possibly did wrong, and in case you tire your subsequent woman pal of being a pathetic sucker, after the number one level of fascination, she could be capable of moreover ditch you. On the opportunity hand, if you put off the errors which you comprehend that you have committed thus far in preceding relationships, your relationship collectively together along with your new partner may be better than with the preceding one. There isn't any quality recipe for achievement, but there are numerous effective techniques to restriction the possibility of failure.

•She wasn't the only

It's now not even the truth that she left due to the truth we screwed it up. She left because of the fact we failed to pick up and examine the indicators she changed into sending us in time. It may be very probably that she best left due to the truth we did now not have capability to go away her in time. Maybe you furthermore may felt that this dating did no longer satisfy you anymore, however the girl have become out to be more potent to stop a relationship that had no future.

www.ingramcontent.com/pod-product-compliance
Lightning Source LLC
Chambersburg PA
CBHW062139020426
42335CB00013B/1259